I HAVE LIVED A THOUSAND YEARS
GROWING UP IN THE HOLOCAUST

LIVIA BITTON-JACKSON

POCKET
BOOKS

LONDON · SYDNEY · NEW YORK

ACKNOWLEDGEMENTS

I wish to express my gratitude to Toni Mendez and Jeanette Smith. Their expert guidance and personal warmth transcended the confines of their function as literary agents and served as a continuous source of inspiration.

My thanks to my editor Stephanie Owens Lurie, and her editorial team, for handling the material for this book with sensitivity and insight and thoughtfulness.

First published in Great Britain by Simon & Schuster UK Ltd, 1999
This edition first published by Pocket Books, 2000
An imprint of Simon & Schuster UK Ltd.
POCKET
BOOKS   A Viacom Company

Copyright © Livia E. Bitton-Jackson, 1999

3 5 7 9 10 8 6 4

Simon & Schuster UK Ltd, Africa House, 64-78 Kingsway, London WC2B 6AH

Simon & Schuster Australia, Sydney.

A CIP catalogue record for this book is available from the British Library

ISBN 07434 08756

Typeset by SX Composing DTP, Rayleigh, Essex
Printed and bound in Great Britain by
Bookmarque Ltd, Croydon, Surrey

CONTENTS

FOREWORD

On 30 April 1995, I took an El-Al flight from Tel Aviv to Munich. From the terminal I took the S-Bahn to Tutzing, and from there I was driven to Seeshaupt, a small Bavarian resort. This was not an easy journey to take, and I took it after some weeks of deliberation. I was going back to Germany – fifty years later.

It was in Seeshaupt on this very day fifty years ago that the American army had liberated me, along with my brother and my mother and thousands of other skeletal prisoners. Some leading citizens of Seeshaupt had decided to commemorate the event. They formed a committee and dispatched letters of invitation to possible survivors all over the world. One such letter reached me in my New York home, and here I was, making a detour, on a Tel Aviv–New York flight, to Seeshaupt.

The former mayor's son, then a nine-year-old boy, remembered how the victorious Allies had led his father and his family and all other members of the local élite to the Seeshaupt train station, where they witnessed a most horrifying picture of human suffering. The sight of thousands of disfigured corpses and

maimed, dying skeletons left an indelible mark on his awareness.

Now he is a doctor in Seeshaupt, and when his patients,
members of the post-war generation, refused to believe his
account of what he saw, he decided to bring back survivors of
that ghastly liberation as living proof that the unbelievable did
happen.

The sky was overcast and a light drizzle veiled my view as
my host, Dr Peter Westebbe, one of the local organizers of the
commemoration, drove me through the streets of Seeshaupt to
the dedication ceremony.

Eighteen survivors had arrived for the ceremony from all
over the world. Some were from the United States, some from
South America, some from Israel, and one from Greece. The
townspeople were there – about three hundred, mostly young.
The present mayor of the town officiated at the dedication of a
monument to those who had died and those who had survived
to be liberated here – over two thousand five hundred, according to records. Young children from the local school planted
trees, danced and sang, and the pastor of the local church
blessed the monument. The local audience was visibly moved.

We, the eighteen survivors who had returned to Seeshaupt,
men and women in their sixties and seventies, briefly remi-
nisced about that liberation day fifty years ago, and as we
looked into each other's eyes, we saw that the years had not
faded the pain of memories. The pain was intact. And so was
the sense of overwhelming burden.

A celebration followed the dedication ceremony. Several hundred guests filled the local beer hall, where tables were set up for
a festive meal and musical entertainment by the local band.

Quietly I slipped out of the hall, and slowly made my way

to the station. Late Sunday afternoon stillness enveloped the small town. I walked along the tracks to the colourless, deserted, memorable platform. No trains. No passengers anywhere. Total emptiness. Only an incessant, light drizzle.

But for me the platform was full. It was brimming with a disarray of sights, hundreds upon hundreds, a bleeding carpet of dead and dying. I saw Greco, the fifteen-year-old Greek boy with enormous, feverish eyes, begging for water. I saw Lilli, the sixteen-year-old brunette with her leg blown off, sitting in a pool of blood. I heard Martha, blinded in both eyes, calling to her mother. And Beth, and Irene . . . ageless faces, skeletal limbs filled the grey, translucent mist.

'There are no more trains today.' I turned round, startled. The woman with the unmistakably Bavarian accent had a pleasant, nondescript face. 'There are no more trains today from this station.'

'Thank you. I'm not waiting for a train.'

She waited, wondering; then, with a hint of suspicion lingering in her manner, she reluctantly walked on.

But the moment was gone. The half-century-old visions were no longer retrievable on the screen of my present reality. A cold, opaque haze enveloped the tracks; the platform and the grim two-storey station house were empty.

I walked back to the beer hall, where the celebration was winding down. 'What message do you have for us?' one of the committee members asked me. 'What lessons?'

I pondered the question. I was fourteen when the war ended, and believed that the evil of the Holocaust was defeated along with the forces that brought it about. Six years later a new life began for me in the New World. A new life, free of threat. A new world, full of hope.

In America I grew from traumatized teen to grandmother-hood. And as the world grew more and more advanced techno-logically, it seemed to grow more and more tolerant of terror and human suffering.

My fears have returned. And yet my hope, my dream, of a world free of human cruelty and violence has not vanished.

My hope is that learning about past evils will help us to avoid them in the future. My hope is that learning what hor-rors can result from prejudice and intolerance, we can cultivate a commitment to fight prejudice and intolerance.

It is for this reason that I wrote my recollections of the hor-ror. Only one who was there can truly tell the tale. And I was there.

For you, the third generation, the Holocaust has slipped into the realm of history, or legend. Or, into the realm of sen-sational subjects on the silver screen. As you read my personal account I believe you will feel – you will know – that the Holocaust was neither a legend nor Hollywood fiction but a lesson for the future. A lesson to help future generations pre-vent the causes of the twentieth-century catastrophe from being transmitted into the twenty-first.

My stories are of gas chambers, shootings, electrified fences, torture, scorching sun, mental abuse, and constant threat of death.

But they are also stories of faith, hope, triumph and love. They are stories of perseverance, loyalty, courage in the face of overwhelming odds and of never giving up.

My story is my message: Never give up.

THE CITY OF MY DREAMS

I dream of enrolling in the prep school in Budapest, the capital city. Budapest is a big, beautiful metropolis with wide streets and tall buildings and yellow trams whizzing around corners. All the streets of Budapest are paved. In our town we have only one paved street, the main street. And it is not wide. We have neither tall buildings, nor trams, only horse-drawn carts and two cars. One of them belongs to my friend's father.

Ours is a small farming town at the edge of the Carpathian foothills. The lovely hills loom in a blue haze towards the west. To the south, the Danube, the cool, rapid river, pulsates with the promise of life. How I love to swim in its clear blue, surging ripples, and lie in the shade of the little forest hugging its banks.

We children splash all summer in the Danube. Families picnic in the grass, the local soccer team has its practice field nearby, and the swimming team trains for its annual meet. Even the army camp empties its sweaty contents once a day, hundreds of recruits, into the cool, cleansing waters of the Danube.

When the sun moves beyond the hills and the

little forest casts a long shadow over the pasture, herds of cattle and sheep arrive at the Danube. The shepherds drive first sheep, then the horses and cows into the water, cursing ever louder, and drive us children out. The mosquitoes arrive, too, with the dusk, and it is time to go home.

The walk through the open pasture is pleasant and cool, but the town is hot and dusty when we reach home. The sheep arrive before us and it is they who churn up the dust. But soon the dust settles, and so does the night. A dark, velvety blanket of silence wraps the town snugly against the intrusion of the outside world. The stars, one by one, light up the dirt roads and the single paved street of the town. By nine o'clock all is quiet. Here and there one hears the bark of a restless dog. Soon the dog, too, will be asleep.

Then the orchestra of insects begins its overture, its harmony disrupted by the discordant croaking of a frog, an inhabitant of a small swamp just beyond the last houses of our street.

I love to lie and daydream for hours after dusk. Life is an exciting mystery, a sweet secret enchantment. In my daydreams I am a celebrated poet, beautiful, elegant, and very talented. My poems open the world's heart to me, and I loll in the world's embrace.

I yearn for my mother's embrace. When, on Sabbath mornings, my friend Bonnie and I join our mothers in the synagogue, Mrs Adler takes Bonnie in her arms and calls her *meine Schönheit*, my beauty, in German. Mrs Adler always says German endearments to Bonnie. Mummy only greets me with a hello and a smile, no hug and no words of endearment.

'That's all nonsense,' Mummy would respond to my complaint. 'Do you want me to call you *meine Schönheit*? Bonnie's mother makes a fool of herself. Why, everyone can see how plain-looking her daughter is!'

What does it matter whether Bonnie is pretty? I care only that Bonnie's mother thinks she is beautiful. And what about the hug?

'I don't believe in cuddling,' Mummy explains with a smile. 'Life is tough, and cuddling makes you soft. How will you face life's difficulties if I keep cuddling you? You're too sensitive as it is. If I would take you in my lap, you'd never want to get off . . . You'd become as soft as butter, unable to stand up to life's challenges.'

Mummy's explanations are unconvincing. I believe she does not hug me because she does not think I am huggable. I believe she does not call me beautiful because she does not think I am pretty. I am too tall and ungainly. My arms and legs are too long, and I keep upsetting things. When I carry a tray of drinks, Mummy shouts at me not to walk so clumsily. That's the reason why everything spills. 'Look at Eva. She's a year younger than you, yet how deftly she carries a tray.' Or 'I was in your friend Julie's house yesterday. You should see how skilfully she helped her mother serve!' Or 'See your brother Bubi? He's a boy, and see how much more he helps out, and how much better he is around the kitchen?'

This I know is the secret of my mother's disapproval: my brother. He is the favourite. He is good. He never answers back, my mother says. And never asks, 'Why do I have to?' whenever she tells him to do this or that. Why can't I be like him?

Why can't I look like him? My brother is good-looking, and I am not. I am far from being pretty. He has curly hair, and I don't. My hair is straight. There is not even an inclination of a wave. 'What a shame!' I hear my mother say to a neighbour.

'Who needs such good looks in a boy? I mixed these two up. My son should've been the girl. And my daughter, her looks would be fine for a boy.'

And there is another thing. My brother Bubi looks like my mother's four brothers. Mummy refers to them as 'my-beautiful-brothers.' The three words as one. Bubi talks like them, he walks like them, and he acts like them. And he is brilliant like they are.

I am like my father's family. They are okay, but they are less dazzling. They are made of much plainer fabric.

Bubi has ability, and I have only ambition. You see, I get good grades because I like to study, but my brother gets good grades without ever opening a book. Mummy is very proud of him. Daddy praises me for my ambition. He says ambition is sometimes more important than ability. You can sometimes accomplish more with ambition than ability.

I wonder: Does the fact that I have ambition mean that I have no natural ability? Or talent? How will I ever become a celebrated poet without talent? Can I get there by ambition alone?

'Look, Elli,' Mummy explains, 'you have a pretty smile, and when you smile, your face becomes quite pretty. Whenever you meet people, say hello with a smile. And people will take you for a pretty girl.'

I listen, and smile whenever I can.

The summer passes and my brother Bubi leaves for Budapest. He is a student at the Jewish Teachers' Seminary there, and I hope and pray that my dream of joining him next year will come true.

Dark, rainy days of autumn freeze into glistening white winter. The gloom of the Hungarian occupation, the slow drag of the war, and increasing food shortages thicken the winter chill. Hitler's shrill radio broadcasts, especially one of his oft-repeated promises, 'We will play football with Jewish heads,' strike panic in my heart. Daddy reassures me. 'Don't worry, little Elli. It's only a manner of speaking. Don't take it literally, God forbid.' Sharp lines of pain etch his square, handsome face as he lets his hand rest on my shoulder. 'Don't even think about these things, Ellike. Just forget you ever heard them.'

But I cannot put the vision out of my mind. Bloody heads rolling on the local soccer field become a recurring nightmare.

As the winter wears on, my father's erect posture begins to stoop somewhat. His silences become longer and the shadows under his cheekbones deeper. Ever since the Hungarian occupation three years ago, when our business was confiscated, Daddy has become more and more distant. His famous wit has become caustic; his laughter, a rare treat. He seems to derive pleasure only from study, and the endless winter evenings find him poring over huge folios of the Talmud.

On my birthday, 28 February, the snow starts to melt. Spring is in the air. Daddy has cheered up a little and it makes my heart sing with joy. I have turned thirteen and it promises to be a wonderful spring. I got a new coat with shoulder pads that make me look less thin and more mature. I look at least fifteen in that wonderful navy coat with high shoulders. Even Jancsi Novák, the heart-throb, smiled at me, and said, 'Oh. Hello.'

Many other wonderful things are happening this spring. I passed the examinations with high marks and Daddy gave his consent. Without wasting a moment, I wrote for application forms to the Jewish Preparatory School in Budapest. I also wrote a long letter to Bubi.

How marvellous it is to see my dreams come into sharper focus with every passing day! How marvellous it is to contemplate living in Budapest, meeting Bubi after school! Going places with him! My brother knows everything about Budapest.

That night my daydreams are not laced with painful longing. They are anticipatory and real, and I fall asleep in a glow of happy excitement.

There is a sharp knock on the window near my bed. In the next room my parents are stirring.

'They are here again,' my father says, in hushed tones. 'I wonder what they want this time?'

'Please be polite to them,' Mummy whispers. 'It's always better to be courteous, even if they are rude. Please. We must avoid trouble.'

I can hear Daddy unbolt the front door. Now there is pounding at the rear entrance of the house.

I hear Daddy quickly rebolt the door and hurry to the back of the house. I hear Mother's footsteps following him.

The illuminated clock says 2.30 a.m.

They always come unexpectedly in the middle of the night, the Hungarian military police. They always come pounding on windows and doors, five or six of them. High-heeled boots, guns perched on shoulders, tall cock feathers tucked in black helmets. They are the dread of the Jews in the occupied territories. They stage raids, *Razzias*, in the middle of the night, looking for concealed weapons. They would turn the house upside down, rudely poke furniture with bayonets, and order Daddy around as if he were a criminal.

'You Jews harbour enemy aliens! You collaborate with the enemy. You want to sell out Hungary to the enemy.'

They would take whatever they liked – packets of coffee,

tea, chocolate. They would open closets and drawers, and slip a watch, a fountain pen, a bracelet, or a silk scarf into their cases.

I was never allowed to get out of bed. Mummy would order me to stay all covered up and pretend to be asleep. But I would always peep and see them menacing my father in rude tones, see my father biting his lips. My father is a tall man, but they would be taller in their feathered helmets. My father is slim and they are sturdy.

They would usually find some violation. Once they officially 'confiscated' my mother's winter coat, saying it was made of English wool – enemy fabric. Another time they took a box of tea, claiming it was Russian tea – enemy import. Once they carted away cartons of soap and cases of cotton thread. It was French soap, American cotton. A severe charge: consorting with the enemy in secret. A summons for the violation was left on the dining-room table, and my father had to appear at the police station the next morning, politely answer an endless row of absurd questions, and sign a 'confession' to the crimes he committed – concealing English wool, French soap, American cotton, Russian tea under Hungarian labels. The fine was steep. Sometimes they detained my father for days. We lived in agony: Are they torturing him? Will they release him alive?

There are voices in the kitchen. Why are they staying in the kitchen so long? Against my mother's orders I tiptoe to the kitchen door and peer through the curtains. There, right in the middle of the kitchen stands my brother, face flushed, talking excitedly to my parents. No one else is in the kitchen. Where are the police?

'Bubi!' My surprise and joy knows no bounds. I rush into the kitchen, barefoot, hugging him. 'Bubi!'

'Shsh. Let's keep still.' My father is pale. 'Let's all sit down. Now, Bubi, tell us, slowly, quietly, what happened.'

The Germans invaded Budapest! On his way to school this morning Bubi saw German tanks roll down Andrassy Ut. He saw a huge flag with a swastika on the Parliament building. He saw a long column of armoured vehicles with Nazi flags move through Budapest's central thoroughfare.

He immediately took a tram to the railway station, bought a ticket, and got on the next train heading for home. He had been travelling since the morning.

My father puts his hand on Bubi's shoulder. 'Son, there must have been some mistake. How could the Germans have invaded Budapest and the whole country know nothing about it? Not a word on the radio. Not a word in the newspapers. How can it be?'

Mummy's voice is tense. 'We will see in the morning. The morning papers will surely headline the news. Then we'll know what to do. Let's go to bed quietly.'

In the morning there is no news of the invasion.

'Bubi, I didn't tell anyone you came home last night. By now I'm sure it was a false alarm. I'm absolutely sure. I don't blame you for being frightened. I don't blame you for coming home. These are frightening times,' Father says softly.

Bubi's eyes catch a strange flame. He says nothing.

'But there's no reason for you to stay at home and miss your classes. I think it's best for you to go right back. There's an express for Budapest at 1 p.m.'

'But, Dad, I saw them – the tanks, the flags with swastikas. Everywhere. And the crowds, I heard them shout, "*Heil* Hitler!"'

'It must've been a demonstration. Some kind of Nazi rally.

. . . If you leave on the 1 p.m. express, you can be on time for classes tomorrow morning. You will have missed only one day of classes.'

Bubi averts his eyes. Father is to be obeyed. Mother concurs and packs a food parcel for my brother.

I kiss my brother goodbye, and a savage stab of pain slashes my insides.

We do not walk him to the station, so as not to arouse suspicion. People would ask questions. And we have no answers.

Bubi leaves for Budapest on the 1 p.m. express.

At 1.20 Mr Kardos, the lawyer down the block whose son also studies in Budapest, comes running to our house. He received a telegram from his son: THE GERMANS INVADED BUDAPEST! He wants to know if we heard anything from Bubi.

Father turns white. 'At this moment my son is on his way back to Budapest.'

'What? He was here? And you knew? You knew and didn't say anything?'

'I did not believe him. No one had heard anything. There was nothing in the papers. On the radio. What shall we do now?'

'I'm going to Budapest at once. To bring home my son.'

For the first time in my life I see my mother cry. She is a strong woman, always cheerful and full of hope. But today she walks about with eyes brimming and red.

My father's face is ashen, and his hands tremble as he lights one cigarette after another.

I want to scream and scream.

The next morning headlines roar: WE ARE LIBERATED! HITLER'S GLORIOUS ARMY IS IN BUDAPEST!

All day long the radio blares 'Deutschland über alles,' and

the country is agog with the news. Two days late. Two days late.

News reaches us of Jews having been arrested in Budapest on the streets, on trams, at their workplaces, at railway stations, and herded into freight trains. And the trains are chained shut. Where were they shipped? No one knows.

Father stops pacing the floor. 'I cannot stand it any longer. There's a train at 8 p.m. I'm going to Budapest to bring Bubi home.'

'It's too late. They'll arrest you, too. You won't be able to help him. Stay here with us. God will be with us, and save him.'

Mother's voice has a strange tremor. I hug her and she begins to cry openly. Father's tall, erect frame crumbles like a dry biscuit. God, if only Bubi were here!

During the night Bubi arrives from Budapest.

Mr Kardos does not return. Neither does his son, Gyuri. They are shipped off in freight trains. They become our first casualties of the Holocaust, together with all the boys and girls of our town who studied in Budapest. They were all taken away from the beautiful Hungarian capital, in trains chained shut, to an unknown destination.

Budapest, the city of my dreams, has become the anteroom of Auschwitz.

'HEY, JEW GIRL, JEW GIRL...'

SOMORJA, 25 MARCH 1944

Almost inaudibly, Mrs Kertész added, 'Goodbye, class. Goodbye, children. You can all go home now.'

Mrs Kertész, our teacher, had just made the shocking announcement: 'Class, the Royal Hungarian Ministry of Education . . . to safeguard our best interests . . . has terminated instruction in all the nation's schools. Effective immediately.' Her voice broke. She swallowed hard. 'Our school is closed, as of now.'

It is Saturday, 25 March 1944. Six days have passed since the Germans invaded Budapest. What about graduation, only three months away? What about our report cards?

But Mrs Kertész leaves the classroom before we have a chance to ask questions. She leaves without a word of reference to the German occupation. Without indication of what is to happen next.

We sit in stunned silence, staring at each other. And then slowly, ever so slowly, my classmates stand up one by one and file out of the classroom.

I, too, rise to my feet and look around. The worn, wood benches bolted to the dark, oil-stained floor.

The whitewashed walls with their threadbare maps and faded pictures. It is all so familiar, so reassuring. Even the dark green crucifix above the door spells security.

For nearly four years I have struggled, sweated, and sometimes triumphed within these walls. In front of this blackboard. For nearly four years I have breathed the smell of the oiled floor mingled with chalk dust, apprehension, and excitement.

Will I ever again sit behind this narrow desk furrowed by a thousand pencil marks? Will I ever again share secrets and moments of hilarity with my classmates?

Perhaps the schools will reopen soon. Perhaps the country will settle down under German occupation and everything will be just as before. I just know that soon everything will be just as before. Lessons will resume and our class will be together again. And we will graduate as planned. I'm quite certain of that.

I decide to leave by the main entrance. The boys use the main entrance. Maybe Jancsi Novák will be leaving just now, too. I want to see him for the last time.

As I turn into the hallway leading to the main entrance, an arm reaches out and blocks my way. I look up, astonished. It is not Novák. A stocky, pimply-faced boy with dark, slicked-back hair stands in my way, grinning. He raises his arm in the Nazi salute and says: '*Heil* Hitler!' A group of boys lining both sides of the stairs echo, '*Heil* Hitler!' Grinning.

I pass through them as I go down the stairs, holding my head high, looking straight ahead. They begin to chant, louder and louder, '*Heil* Hitler! *Sieg Heil! Sieg Heil! Sieg Heil!*'

I run down the stairs. The stocky boy shouts, 'Down with the Jews! Down with the Jews!' And the others echo, louder and louder, 'Down with the Jews! Down with the Jews!'

I fly down the stairs and out to the street. I run and run. Other sounds reach me. I recognize these sounds. My schoolmates are singing the vulgar army marching song: '*Hej, zsidó lány, zsidó lány* . . .' Hey, Jew girl, Jew girl . . . I am far down the block now and I still hear them singing the repulsive popular tune.

The sounds follow me home. Mocking, taunting, devastating. Sounds that penetrate. Sounds that bruise. Sounds that can kill. As I run, one of my plaits comes undone. Tears choke my throat. Sweat runs down my back. My temples throb.

No one is at home. It is Sabbath morning and my parents are still at the synagogue. I fish the house key from under the mat and slam the great heavy oak door behind me. I run to my room and bury my face in my pillow. My stomach trembles with every convulsive sob.

I weep and weep. I weep for my classroom, which is no longer my classroom. For the school that will never be my school again. I weep for my life, which will never be the same.

THE TALE OF THE YELLOW BICYCLE

SOMORJA, 27 MARCH 1944

The dreaded moment has come: There is no escape. We are in the hands of the SS. The process of our 'liquidation' has begun.

We are lost and helpless. Like lifeless matter we are carried along on a powerful conveyor belt towards an unknown fate. The smooth operation of the process is strangely reassuring.

It is easiest to give up. The struggle is over. Perhaps it is God's will. No, not perhaps. Surely it is God's will.

On a Monday morning in March, all Jews are ordered to appear at the town hall to be registered. We have to line up to be counted, and we are supplied with tags. Like children leaving for summer camp. Or pets leaving the pet shop.

We are ordered to deliver all our valuables – jewellery, radios, and vehicles.

I have to part with my new Schwinn bicycle.

My bike is my only real possession. It had been a birthday present from my parents. For years I had hoped and prayed for a bike, and my new Schwinn is more wonderful than anything I had imagined. More grand.

It is bright yellow, with red-and-yellow webbing on the back wheel. It has a dark-yellow leather seat and the shiny chrome handlebars are tucked into handles that match the seat. It is beautiful.

At first I think I will not be able to give up my bicycle. How can they tell me to take it to the town hall and just leave it there, my most precious possession? Without a sound of protest. Without even demanding an explanation. I thought such things could not happen.

My father's face was frozen into a mask of defiance when he brought the news to us on Sunday afternoon. I began to scream. I was not going to do it! Let them kill me, I was not going to let them take my new bike! I had not even ridden it yet. I had been waiting for spring to try it out. Spring was just beginning. The snow had just begun to melt, and as soon as the mud cleared I was going to take my brand new shiny Schwinn on the street. I could not part from it now!

In my panic and rage I felt helpless, exposed. Violated.

Father spoke to me in a low tone, almost a whisper. His voice was choked with anger and pain. 'As soon as this is over, all this madness, I will buy you another Schwinn. Never mind this one, Elli. Never mind. You will have the most beautiful bike money can buy. A full-size bike. Bigger than this one and even more beautiful.'

'I don't want another bike. I have not even tried this one out. What right do they have to take it from me? You gave it to me. It was my birthday present. It's mine. How can they just *take* it?'

Daddy's soft hands on my cheeks soothed my sobbing. He repeated, over and over, 'Never mind, Ellike. Never mind.'

On Monday morning, as I walk, tall and erect, with my

Schwinn, between my father and my brother, each pushing his own bicycle, I feel no more rage or panic. Only pain, and humiliation. But when I see my bright, shiny bike lined up against the wall among the many battered, lacklustre old bicycles, I feel the ground slip under me.

In a daze I follow Daddy and my brother to the courtyard of the town hall. Jewellery, silverware, radios, and cameras are piled high on long tables. Mummy waits in line to place some of her best silver cutlery and her antique silver candelabra on top of the pile. I do not look at her face. But I see the other faces as they turn from the table after depositing their precious objects. Degradation and shame flickers in every eye.

That night Father takes me down into the cellar. In the far corner of the dank, dark underground room the flashlight reveals a rough spot on the earthen floor.

'Look, Elli. Here on this spot I buried our most precious pieces of jewellery, about twenty-five centimetres deep. Mummy and Bubi also know the spot. Each one of us should know where the jewels are buried. We don't know which one of us will return. Will you remember?'

I refuse to look. 'I don't want to know! I don't want to remember!'

Daddy put his arm about my shoulders. 'Elli . . . Ellike . . .' he repeats softly. Then, slowly, with weighty footsteps, he leads me up the stairs.

In the kitchen Mummy turns from the stove and asks Daddy in a matter-of-fact tone, 'Have you shown her?'

With a silent nod Daddy intends to forestall any further discussion on the subject. But I burst out crying. 'Why should Daddy show me the spot? Why? Why should I know about the jewels? Why? Tell me, why? Tell me! I don't want to know the spot! I don't want to be the one to survive! I don't want to survive alone! Alone, I don't want to live. Oh, God, I don't want to live if you don't! I don't want to know about anything! I don't want to know!'

Dead silence follows my outburst. My sobs are the only sounds in the kitchen. In utter misery I go to my room. I pull the blanket over my head to muffle my convulsive screams.

Oh, God. Why? Why? Why?

The Tale of the Yellow Star

The sound of the town crier wakes me. Before, my fascination with the town crier's performance had been voracious. I would always be in front of the townsfolk who gathered on the small hill near our house upon hearing his drumbeat. I stood close to the stocky man in his green uniform and cap so that I could watch his distinctive ritual. At the conclusion of the drumbeat he would, in one motion, thrust the drumsticks into the wide leather strap on his shoulder then yank out a document, while contorting his face into a vocal instrument. His mouth turned to one side and opened round like a trumpet so that he could blast the proclamation. The syllables erupted like bullets from a pistol. At the conclusion of the recital the audience would quickly disperse, but I could not stop gaping as the town crier reversed the process, turning his trumpet mouth back into a puffy, round visage, while tucking the sheet of paper under his shoulder strap, yanking out the drumsticks and striking his drum with the barrage of a rapid-fire march. It was only then that I would reluctantly walk back home.

This time I do not go to the square. Lately the

town crier's proclamations bring bad news for us. News that humiliates me in front of the other listeners. I open my window and let the words filter in through the muslin curtains.

'Hear ye! Hear ye! As of 8 a.m. this Tuesday morning, the twenty-eighth day of the month of March, in the nineteen hundred and forty-fourth year of our Lord Jesus Christ, all the Jews must wear a yellow star on the left side of the chest. The star must be of canary-yellow fabric, of six equal points, eight centimetres in diameter. Any Jew – man, woman, or child – seen on the street without the star shall be arrested!

'Likewise, a canary-yellow, six-pointed star of one metre in diameter shall be painted on the exterior wall to the left of the main entrance of every Jewish residence. As of 8 a.m. this Tuesday morning, the twenty-eighth day of the month of March, in the nineteen hundred and forty-fourth year of our Lord Jesus Christ, the residents of any Jewish house not duly marked with the afore-indicated star shall be arrested!

'This proclamation be duly . . .'

I shut the window. My God, what next? A yellow star? In after-school Hebrew class I had heard evil tales of Jews having to wear humiliating markings on their clothes, long, long ago, in the Middle Ages. The Jew badge.

This yellow star was a Jew badge!

I refuse to leave the house. I was not going to appear with the Jew badge. I couldn't be seen wearing that horrible, horrible thing. I would die if any of my schoolmates saw me.

My brother makes a brave joke of the whole thing. He makes believe he has been awarded a medal. He cuts a star out of cardboard and covers it with glistening golden-yellow silk fabric. It really looks like a gold military medal. He pins it on his chest and marches about the streets with a smile of triumph.

My brother's 'medal' becomes the envy of his friends. Soon other young boys begin wearing decorative yellow stars, pretending to be honoured and not humiliated by the star. They, with my brother in the lead, see it as a mark of distinction.

I could not understand them. When I saw my tall, handsome, seventeen-year-old brother wearing his 'medal' with mock pride, his valiant attempt to turn humiliation into triumph made me want to cry. It was a bitter, bitter joke. My anger was laced with raw pain.

I do not leave the house for nearly a week. Mummy pleads, her voice gentle and sad, 'Elli, let's thank God for being alive. Let us thank God for being together, in our own house. What's a yellow star on a jacket? It does not kill or condemn. It does not harm. It only says you're a Jew. That's nothing to be ashamed of. We're not marked for being criminals. Only for being Jews. Aren't you proud of being a Jew?'

I don't know if I am proud to be a Jew. I had never thought about it. But I know I do not want to be marked as a Jew or as anything else. I am hurt and outraged at being made to wear a glaring label, a thing intended to set me apart and humiliate me. A criminal, or Jew, what's the difference in their intent? What's the difference in my shame? I am no longer a human being. I am singled out at will, an object.

Daddy seems oblivious to the star. Mummy has to remind him to put on his jacket with the star every time he goes outdoors. You cannot simply pin a star on whatever you are wearing. The law stipulates that a star has to be sewn on to every garment. With small stitches, to be exact. Mummy solves this problem by sewing stars to several of our outer garments, and we could choose to wear only these when going outdoors.

The canary-yellow star does not detract from Daddy's

elegance. He was always impeccably dressed and had a proud bearing, and even with the badge of shame he continues to exude an air of quiet dignity. His lack of awareness of this degrading emblem puzzles me. How can he so totally ignore the star?

The grating, high-pitched tones of the town crier's chant carry a new message. End-of-the-year report cards are being distributed at all the local schools. As none of the nation's schools will reopen, all schoolchildren, from first-years to secondary school seniors, must appear in person at the respective schools to pick up their report cards, diplomas, certificates of graduation. Each graduate of the municipal secondary school must appear in person at the institute at ten o'clock this very morning to receive his or her diploma.

That's me! That's us! Our diplomas will be handed out. The entire class will be there. It will be like a graduation, a class reunion! I am thrilled.

Then I remember the star. My heart sinks. I go to my wardrobe, and there, on my blue spring jacket, left of the zipper, is the horrible thing. When I put it on, it looks even larger.

What if I meet the gang who had menaced me and shouted '*Heil* Hitler' into my face nine days ago, on the day the school abruptly closed?

Even worse, what if I meet Jancsi Novák? What would he say to me? Would he be embarrassed at the now obvious difference between us?

I hang the jacket back in my wardrobe.

'Coward.'

It is my brother.

'I am not. I am not a coward.'

'Then what are you? Why haven't you left the house for nearly a week? And now, your report card. Even your diploma. I know what they mean to you. But you're afraid to wear the star. Isn't that cowardice?'

No one is going to call me a coward. I snatch the jacket and run out of the house without saying goodbye to my brother.

Once I am outside, brilliant sunshine splashes into my face. The acacia tree in front of our house is the brightest green I have ever seen. But my enjoyment of the outdoors is ruined by the sight of the glaring yellow star near the front entrance. The huge painted shape is larger and more grotesque than I had visualized.

I break into a run. I remove my jacket as soon as I reach the school building and carry it folded inside out, hiding the star. The corridors are empty. Report-card distribution is already in progress in every classroom.

In mine, Mrs Kertész is addressing the class. She is saying farewell. With tears in her eyes she wishes us all success and tells us of her plan to retire early and return to her native town in Upper Slovakia. We drink in her words with the thirst of those who know that this is the last few drops of their water supply.

Mrs Kertész starts distributing the report cards together with the diplomas – alphabetically.

My name is called and I approach her desk. Mrs Kertész pauses. 'Class,' she says, 'Elvira Friedmann received . . .' My heart gives a jolt and begins to pound in a wild rhythm. My temples throb. I do not hear her words. But I know. A moment later I am clutching the coveted honour scroll. It had been an unattainable dream. Words precipitate from the fog. 'Congratulations. We are happy for you, Elvira.'

In a state of delirium I walk to my seat, past a multitude of glances of shared happiness and hands protruding into the aisle, squeezing, touching, slapping, embracing. I have a heady feeling of joy. Of gratitude. Bliss. Is this really happening?

Then it is all over. Final goodbyes. Final embraces. Promises. Tears.

I head for home, still in a glow of unreality. A cold breeze greets me at the school's exit, and I absently put on my jacket.

'Congratulations.' I am startled by a deep voice behind me. I turn sharply, and stare into the smiling face of Jancsi Novák. 'You received the class honour scroll. Congratulations.'

'Thank you. How did you know? The scroll, I mean. I mean, that I got the honour scroll.' Suddenly, I remember the star on my jacket, and blush. It is too late. He must have seen it already. But in his facial expression there is no hint that he noticed the star. Not a flicker.

'I saw the list. Your name was posted on the honour roll,' he said, still smiling warmly.

'Honour roll? Where?'

'In the central corridor, on the wall. Under the picture of Horthy and the flag. I spotted your name in the girls' column.'

I blush again. 'I didn't know about the honour roll. They had never posted the names before.'

'This year it's different. This year there won't be any yearbook. Posting takes the place of the yearbook.' He pauses. He is no longer smiling. 'This year everything is different. No yearbook. No graduation. Nothing.' Then a cheerful thought lights up his handsome, masculine features. 'Well, not quite nothing. We received the honour scroll, didn't we?'

'You, too? Congratulations!' He is pleased with my enthusiasm. And I walk on air.

We reach the front entrance of our house. We did not meet anyone. Nothing mars the perfect moments. Jancsi stretches out his hand. 'Good luck. Will I see you again? I will be coming to Somorja every Thursday. To the library. In the afternoon. Perhaps I could see you there?' As he shakes my hand, his glance falls on the yellow star. All at once, his eyes hold unfathomable sadness. It astounds me. Then he averts his gaze from the star. I promise to meet him at the library next Thursday afternoon. But the glow is gone. Suddenly, I feel unbearably bruised. His sadness is too much to bear.

Farewell, Old Mr Stern

SOMORJA, 5–18 APRIL 1944

I never saw Jancsi Novák again. On Wednesday morning the town crier announced that 'Jews are forbidden under penalty of immediate arrest to have intercourse of any kind with Christians. Jews are forbidden under penalty of immediate arrest to greet, acknowledge greeting from, speak to, correspond with, deliver to, or receive objects from Christians. Christians are enjoined to observe the same. Jews are forbidden under penalty of immediate arrest to enter public places – theatres, cinemas, restaurants, cafés, schools, parks, the post office, city hall or library. Christians are enjoined to report any Jew seen entering the aforementioned places.'

We are virtually under house arrest. I dread meeting neighbours on the street. I walk stiffly, averting my gaze from every face in fear of breaking the law. What if I forget and say hello? Or respond to a friend's hello? And what if . . . we don't forget? What then? Would we pass each other like strangers? But that's not possible.

It is. Our neighbours and friends pass us unacknowledged, unrecognized, unseen. The awkwardness I have feared never arose. Our Christian friends and neighbours seem to have no conflict in observing the restrictions. My sense of isolation is overwhelming.

My God, have we been reduced to lifeless ghosts?

Eight days later another drumbeat, another announcement. The one we have dreaded most.

All Jews of Somorja are to be removed from the town and concentrated in a ghetto in another town – Nagymagyar, fourteen kilometres from here. In five days every Jewish family in Somorja must stand ready for deportation to the ghetto. Every Jewish family may take to the ghetto personal possessions and one room of furniture. Everything else must be left behind, exactly as is. Keys must be delivered to police headquarters prior to departure.

GHETTO! I had read about the ghetto, a horrible, horrible place. Jews lived in ghettos during the Dark Ages. My God, are we descending into the Dark Ages?

Five more days. The weather has turned from late spring to early summer and the fragrance of violets fills the air. Five days of feverish packing. What to take? What to leave behind?

The cock-feathered military police arrive and our belongings are laden on peasant carts under their surveillance. Foodstuffs, pieces of furniture, clothing, firewood. Mother supervises the operation. She organizes the proper packing of each cart, talks to the police, calms my father. Tension has converted him into a statue of stone. I am doubled up with an excruciating stomach-ache. Mummy's sister, Aunt Serena, who lives at the other end of town, moves about in a daze. My brother Bubi is the only help Mummy has. He is like Mummy, practical and efficient. We have to hurry. By 1 p.m. Somorja must be *judenrein*, free of Jews.

It is eleven o'clock. All carts are laden. Father is sitting on the furniture cart. Aunt Serena is on the cart with the clothing and food. Bubi also hops on to the cart. The coachmen snap their whips and the carts are off. Mummy and I wave goodbye to them, and my heart sinks.

Mummy and I will follow them on the cart with the firewood. Mummy wants to go to the cemetery first, to take leave of her parents' tombs. She has received permission from the police.

Mummy's parents died before I was born and are buried in the old Jewish cemetery, near the next village, a forty-minute walk. My grandfather was a revered Hebrew scholar and a *tzaddik*. My grandmother was known for her beauty and for her friendly, cheerful personality. I have always regretted not having known them. I know only their graves. I used to accompany Mummy to the cemetery whenever she visited their graves. And now I am to accompany her again, perhaps for the last time.

The cart with the firewood stands in front of our house, waiting until we return.

'Your keys.' The grim cock-feather policeman extends his hand. 'Hand over the keys.'

'Ah, yes. The keys.' Mummy's embarrassment is painful. I avert my eyes. 'You want them now? Can it wait until we get back from the cemetery? We won't be long. We will be back before the deadline. Before one o'clock. Can I give you the keys then?'

'Now.'

Mummy hands the keys to the stern figure. And in her eyes there is a veiled look of humiliation and terror.

Mummy and I hurry along the length of our town, past

wide-open gates through which men and women, driven by fear, hastily carry a hotch-potch of belongings and load them on to the carts. They do not take time to cast a glance in our direction.

We, too, hurry on. We pass the synagogue at the end of the town. Old Mr Stern stands facing the western wall of the synagogue, deep in prayer. Mummy motions to me, and we stand still, waiting for him to finish his prayer. Mr Stern closes his prayer book in slow motion, and bends to the wall, kissing it. Tears flow down his white beard.

For several moments Mummy and I watch the old man stand there with eyes closed, clinging to the wall of the synagogue. The old man and the wall are one.

We approach him quietly. Mummy touches him lightly on the shoulder. 'Mr Stern. Farewell. God be with you.'

The old man is motionless.

'Mr Stern. The prayer. We, too, want to pray,' Mummy says softly. 'What shall we pray?'

His head turns, but his eyes remain locked in a realm far beyond us, beyond the desolation of the synagogue yard. 'We are going far, far away. On a very long road. Perhaps it will never end.' Mr Stern's sobs become audible. 'We must pray. The prayer for the road. The road is ahead of us . . . It's very, very long.' His voice is drowned in convulsive sobs. Mummy takes him by the arm and leads him into his house right behind the synagogue.

As we approach the cemetery I can see the tombstones glistening white in the brilliant sunshine. I lie down in the grass among the graves, pressing my aching belly against the moist ground. The murmur of Mummy's prayer dulls the pain in my stomach. It's 12.30 p.m. We must hurry back.

On the main street all carts are gone. The gates of the Jewish houses are wide open. I can see scattered furniture, pots, and pans, lying about in the yards, doorways, and even on the pavement. But no living soul. Where are the Gentile neighbours? Their windows and doors are shut. Shades are drawn in every window.

There is only one solitary cluster of life in town. The lonely horse cart in front of our house laden with firewood, the horse impatiently flicking its tail, the driver frozen in his seat, and the cock-feathered policemen menacingly pacing the pavement. It's five minutes to one. Two Jewish females are still on the loose in otherwise pure 'Aryan' Somorja.

Without a word Mother gets on the cart next to the driver. I climb on to the small seat fixed at the back facing the pile of firewood. The peasant cracks his whip, *'Gyutteee!'* and the horse and wagon roll on to the open road. A sharp stab of pain slashes my stomach. From the bend in the road I can see the yellow star on our house recede into the distance.

I cannot see the road ahead. I am facing the past as it slips into oblivion. The steel-spiked cart wheels churn up a cloud of dust sprinkled with tiny pebbles. My birthplace is disappearing rapidly. Will I ever see it again?

Finally the narrow dirt road widens into the main street of Nagymagyar. The cart comes to a halt in front of the synagogue yard, a small enclave for twenty families enclosed by a tall wire fence. This is the ghetto.

Over five hundred families are crowded into the yard. Every family brought the allocated amount of furniture, food, clothing and personal effects. There is no room for any of it. Neither is there room for the people herded in here from fifteen communities of the region. People are helplessly standing and milling about – mothers and infants, elderly men and women, small children.

Father, Aunt Serena and Bubi, who arrived before us, are there, surrounded by heaps of furniture, bundles of clothes, pots and pans, mattresses, prams, sacks of flour, and metal stoves.

'That's the sofa from our salon!' A girl about my age is pointing to a deep scarlet satin corner protruding from the heap. Where are my favourite dining-room chairs with the Gobelin seats? They must be somewhere in this mountain of furniture.

By nightfall the yard clears of people. Every available spot is utilized. People crowd into toolsheds, storage rooms, attics, basements, cellars, stairwells, and into the synagogue itself. Only the mountain of precious belongings remains in the middle of the yard.

Our family has been assigned to share two tiny rooms and a tiny kitchen in a small house with a family named the Blumenfelds. We manage to fit a folding bed in the kitchen for my brother to sleep on. Father, Mother, Aunt Serena, and I sleep in one room, the Blumenfelds in the other. Mummy and I share the bed, Aunt Serena sleeps on a narrow sofa, and Father on an even narrower folding bed.

We are lucky. In other houses six, seven, or eight families are squeezed in together. To make room, baths, stoves, and washbasins are removed and put out in the yard; kitchens and bathrooms, even toilets serve as living quarters. Beds are everywhere. Simply everywhere. It's hilarious.

There are beds even in the synagogue entrance hall. Those who sleep in the synagogue itself have to rise before the morning prayers, and wait until after the evening prayers before they can retire for the night. I think this is rather convenient. You simply have to poke your nose from under the covers, and you are in the synagogue for morning prayers!

'You should live in the synagogue,' I say to my brother. 'Your problems would be solved.'

My brother has trouble getting up for early-morning prayers. You have to jerk his covers off; nothing else works in waking him. Then it's a long sleepy drag until he makes it to the synagogue, usually late. Here, with one foot off the bed, he can join the prayers on time.

Most of life's activities take place in the yard. Here several women are cooking on one stove. There a mother is bathing three children in a tub. A long line forms before the public toilet, another one before the public bath. And, alongside the tall wire fence, a row of Hungarian soldiers and military police are watching the spectacle. They are our guards.

In the beginning I felt self-conscious of their stares. But gradually they have melted into the present scenery, and the awkwardness has waned.

Our life is taking on a bearable course. The early confusion changed into a harmonious hustle and bustle. Together we prepare meals, eat at long tables, retire for the night, and rise for prayers. The mood is shifting to optimistic, even confident. There is a hopeful tone to the rhythm of life. The worst is over. We have been uprooted from our homes; our property was confiscated; we have been humiliated, herded and crowded like cattle into an enclosure, stared at from behind a fence like animals in a zoo. Yet God in His mercy made it all manageable. And bearable. We know we are not cattle or captured beasts in a zoo. We have carved a dignified lifestyle out of our confines. We are going to make it. We *are* making it!

I learn to like the ghetto. Here I have met more people I can identify with than ever before. Girls my age. Good-looking boys just a little older than me. Well-dressed ladies. Impressive men. Adorable children.

And they are all so exposed to you. Their intimate habits are open to your observation. Families at their dinner table, families washing before bed, families playing with their children, mothers suckling their infants, fathers studying with their sons, embraces, scoldings, tears, laughter, cries of pain and joy. And lines for the toilet. All in the synagogue yard.

I relish it all. I am part of every life. And every life is part of mine. I'm a limb of a larger body.

I enjoy the toilet line most. It's long and slow-moving. One has time to connect, and talk. There's so much to learn. So many people with so many stories.

For the first time in my life, I am happy to be a Jew. And I am happy to share this peculiar condition of Jewishness. The handsome boys, lively women, beautiful babies, grey-bearded old men – all in the same yard of oppression, together.

The cock-feathered policemen who had trampled on our sofas and our self-esteem, the Gentile neighbours who were afraid to say goodbye, the Jancsi Nováks, the kind, gentle friends who have not attempted to send a note of sympathy, the peasant wagon drivers who dutifully accepted wages from us for delivering us to the enemy, the villagers who lined the roads and watched the carts taking us to the prison compound and kept their silence . . . they all are on the other side of the fence. A tall fence separates us. A world separates us because they do not understand.

But we, on this side of the fence, we understand. We put up sheets around tubs in the yard in order to take baths. We cook on open stoves. We stand in long lines for the toilet. No friend-ship or love binds as this deep, spontaneous, easy mutuality.

I fall in love again in the ghetto. His name is Pinhas. He's a tall, thin, pale boy with large dark eyes.

One day, as I sit in the yard on a pile of firewood and write, I notice him watching me. I am copying my poems into a note-book I brought from home.

I have over one hundred poems. My first poem, about a ship tossed by angry waves on a stormy sea, attracted my teacher's attention and she included it in the annual Mother's Day con-cert programme. I recited it to an appreciative audience, and became an instant celebrity of sorts at the age of eight. The epithet 'poet' was added to my name, and I was invited to recite my poetry at all kinds of public functions.

Being a 'poet' is central to my self-image, my aspirations and dreams. I write about nature, historical figures, my moods. I write almost constantly, often feverishly.

My poems are all very sad. Pain is their common denominator.

'Why? Why all this *Weltschmerz?*' Mummy would ask, somewhat puzzled, somewhat indignant. 'Why don't you write cheerful little verses about trees, birds, kittens? Why the lurking tragedy behind every blade of grass?'

'Because she is a true poet,' Father would reply. 'The true poet knows life is laced with pain. Human life is fashioned for tragedy.'

My poems have been scribbled on scraps of paper, and now I am copying them all into one notebook. I work at it for hours daily, when not helping Mummy with the cooking, or playing with children, or standing in lines.

At first I think Pinhas is watching me out of curiosity. But then I catch him watching me from behind the synagogue entrance when he is supposed to be inside, praying. I am not writing then. I am peeling potatoes.

The next time I see him, I smile at him and he smiles back. I am in love. And when my best friend Bobbi says he looks interesting, I can barely contain my happiness. 'Interesting' is top evaluation.

Pinhas becomes central to my existence. I anticipate meeting him in lines, watch for him as he goes to shul, look for him in the yard. A glimpse of Pinhas seems to pale everything else.

I take to endless hair brushing, experimenting with new styles. My hair is my strong point.

Mummy was disappointed when I turned out blonde. She had hoped for dark-haired, dark-eyed children, and both my brother and I are blond with blue-green eyes. But at least my brother has curly hair, which Mummy had hoped for. My hair is as straight as freshly combed linen. 'And as the rays of sun,' my aunt Celia used to add. But that's Aunt Celia, and not Mummy. Mummy had always been disappointed with my hair. It's only recently that she has started to approve, even admire my hair.

'Just let it hang down,' she advises. 'It's most striking that way. Just let it hang in two plaits, it's best. Nobody has hair as long as yours, or as rich in texture. Or as brilliantly blonde. Just let it simply hang down in plaits.'

She likes nothing else about me. But my hair makes up for it, I think. Thank God for my hair.

I try to roll the plait around my head. It makes me look older. It's not becoming, however. Finally, I hit on a style. I crisscross the plaits at the back, tying each end with a ribbon to the other side at the neck. It's quite striking. I wonder if Pinhas will notice the difference.

He sees me a little later, on my way to the well. He stops in his tracks, and does a double-take. And smiles. He stands without moving, and his eyes follow me to the line, and all the way as I carry the pail of water back to the stove. I almost drop the pail from excitement.

My day is made. I help around the house cheerfully, not objecting even to kneading the dough. The trough is set up in the yard and I can watch people while I work.

'And people can watch my little sister and see that she's working hard. Isn't that the idea?'

I ignore my brother's remark. I'm anxious to catch another

glimpse at Pinhas. My world is filled with newfound excitement. Perhaps next time he'll speak to me. We will become friends. It's all very, very exciting.

Rumours reach the ghetto. Rumours of an impending 'liquidation' . . . of deportation to internment camps, labour camps, concentration camps. According to reports, other ghettos have already been liquidated and their inhabitants taken by train to camps somewhere in Austria.

There are other rumours, too. Younger men, from eighteen to forty-five, are being rounded up and sent to the Russian front to dig ditches for the Germans.

With every rumour Aunt Serena seems to shrink deeper and deeper into herself. She has changed since we left home. Her good-natured humour is gone. Her calm, patient smile is gone. And she has stopped singing. I used to love to listen to her voice – a soft, melodious, warm voice. Daddy used to tease her that she sang every song as if it were a lullaby.

Now she is silent. Silent and sad, and withdrawn, like a singing bird snatched from her nest and locked up in a cage. The ghetto is her cage. The sudden veil of gloom which has settled over her every aspect seems to grow heavier with every piece of threatening news. She barely talks. On Friday nights she does not even seem to hear the kiddush, only stare silently into the candlelight. As if she left her soul in her nest, her simple, charming home on the outskirts of Somorja, my favourite hiding-place.

'Don't worry, my dear sister.' Mummy puts her arms about her. 'It will be over soon. Soon all this will pass, like a bad dream.'

Mummy's words of comfort suddenly, inexplicably, fill my heart with fear.

A Miracle

'I'm glad they are taking us to labour camps,'
Mummy remarks in response to the rumours. 'Our
food is almost gone. At least we can work for our
food. Here they don't let us get even a loaf of bread!'
Mummy, always practical and optimistic, makes us
all feel better about the rumours.

But how will we obtain food in the meantime?

The ghetto was totally isolated. Ghetto residents
were forbidden to leave; people on the outside were
forbidden to enter. They were forbidden even to
approach the fence.

What will happen when we run out of food?

Days pass and we use up the last scrapings. Our
flour sack is empty. This morning I kneaded bread
from the last batch of flour.

There is a commotion at the front gate. People
run past our room towards the front. Something is
going on at the fence. I quickly join them to see what
the furore is about.

There is always something going on. Yesterday a
baby was born. The day before someone got a letter
from the Budapest ghetto.

Outside the gate a buxom peasant woman is

arguing with the young soldier on guard. She insists on entering the ghetto, but the soldier refuses to allow her to come near the gate. The woman is making a great fuss, angrily scolding the young guard. I know that soldier. The other day he called out to me and asked my name. I told him my name even though I knew it was not permitted. But he looked kind. And very young. He had soft brown eyes, and blond fuzz for a moustache. He told me he was from a small town beyond the Danube, and I answered I was from Somorja.

All at once I catch sight of a girl in part obliterated by the buxom woman still in the midst of her shouting match with the guard.

'Márta!'

Márta Kálmán, my schoolmate from Somorja, hears my shout. She is at the fence in a flash.

'Elli! Ellike!' Her face is flushed with excitement. 'Oh, Elli, I can't believe we found you!'

She runs and frantically tugs at her mother's sleeve. 'Mother! Mother! Look! It's Ellike! She's there. Come, quick!' Unceremoniously she drags the irate woman away from the soldier, towards me.

Now I recognize Mrs Kálmán. She used to drive Márta in her buggy from their farm to our house. I used to help Márta with German and maths.

When she sees me, Mrs Kálmán practically charges the fence. She thrusts her arms through the bars and grabs my hand, shaking it forcefully. The young guard catches up with her.

'You can't do that. It's against the rules.'

All at once the guard catches sight of me.

'Good morning.'

'Good morning. These are my friends. May I talk to them for a few minutes?'

'OK, but be careful. Just a few minutes.'

'Oh, Ellike. I'm so happy to see you. We thought they killed you, all of you. And here you are. My God!'

'Hush, girl,' Mrs Kálmán warns her daughter. 'We brought you some things. Flour, eggs, and a goose. We owe you so much. You know, Márta passed her maths, and in German she got a high mark! We would have brought you these things sooner, but we didn't know where to find you. They wouldn't tell us anything.'

The young guard is agitated. The other soldiers stationed further alongside the fence begin to take notice of the hubbub. A huge crowd has gathered on the inner side of the fence.

'Please. They must leave now.'

'Officer, I brought some things for this young lady. She's my daughter's best friend. Can I give them to her?'

The guard casts a hurried, frightened glance at me. My eyes reflect a desperate plea.

'Be quick. Don't let anyone see.'

Márta and her mother carry the things from the cart at a run. The live goose and the white bundle containing at least two dozen eggs fit between the bars. A sack of flour is hurled above the fence, landing on the shoulder of a young boy, who quickly carries it to our lodgings. Mrs Kálmán's arms draw me into an awkward embrace from behind the bars. 'God be with you, Miss Friedmann. God be with you!'

Márta cries unabashedly.

The goose in my arms feels warm, and brings on a rush of memories. Bittersweet memories of fluffy white geese in our yard. Lovely goslings I had held in my lap. Memories of another era.

Choked with emotion and chagrin, I manage to whisper thanks to the young guard. As I carry my precious cargo to our lodgings, a large admiring crowd of men, women, and children accompany me. They all join in the celebration of the miracle they witnessed at the gate.

Thank you, God, for this miracle. For your providence.

Thank you, God, for the miracle of human kindness.

DADDY, HOW COULD YOU LEAVE ME?

NAGYMAGYAR, 14 MAY 1944

We never got to use any of the food supplies the Kálmáns brought after all. The end approached sooner than we expected.

After midnight there is a loud knock on the door of the small apartment.

'Mr Friedmann Markus is to appear at the gate immediately.'

Daddy is fully awake. He dresses in haste, and hurries to the gate of the ghetto. He identifies himself, and the guard hands him a telegram. It is a summons for him to go to a forced-labour camp in Komárom some fifty kilometres away. He is to report at the gate at 5 a.m. tomorrow morning.

Every man between the ages of eighteen and forty-five received a similar summons during the night.

News of the summonses sends a shock wave throughout the ghetto. Rumours are turning into reality. Military trucks roar into the square and helmeted police pour out of the vehicles, quickly surrounding the ghetto with guns drawn, ready for action. What action? What's going to happen? Is this the beginning of 'liquidation'?

Grim and tight-lipped, Mother is packing Daddy's knapsack. Mummy was looking forward to the labour camp, but did not think Daddy would be taken away from us. The suddenness of it all, the military police with guns drawn . . . it does not bode well.

I hear Mummy moving about in the darkened room, packing wordlessly. Daddy is in the kitchen, talking to my brother in a low murmur. As I huddle in bed, my stomach is twisted in knots like a rubber hose.

'Mummy, if I fall asleep, will you wake me at four thirty? Do you promise? Please, Mummy . . .'

'OK, OK. I'll wake you. Just go to sleep.'

My head, the only part of me free of stomach-ache, is whizzing with a million thoughts. Daddy had called me into the kitchen and told me to take care of Mummy.

'Don't be frightened, Elli,' he said. 'The Almighty is going to be with you all. He will take care of my family. You're a strong girl, Elli. Remember to help Mummy in every way.' He took my face in his two gentle yet muscular hands and drew it slowly to his own. Time stood still, and I thought my heart would break. I wanted to speak, but my words drowned in a morass of pain and helplessness. I wanted to tell him how much I loved him. I wanted to tell him that I knew he loved me. I wanted to tell him that I knew he thought I had nice legs and that it made me happy and proud. I wanted to tell him that our long walks, our long, silent walks together, were the happiest times of my life. And our swimming together in the Danube on the long, hot summer afternoons, were the happiest afternoons of my life. I wanted to tell him how I loved him for his fast walk and powerful swimming, for his silences, for his athletic figure, for his youthful, quick movements. But I did not speak. I could not bridge that distance with words. I held him very tight, my hands gripping his slim torso, my face buried in his neck. I did not cry. I was numb with the horrible foreknowledge of finality.

Gently, he loosened my grip. 'Go to sleep now, Ellike. It is very late.'

'Daddy, I want to speak to you in the morning. I want to tell you something.'

'OK. In the morning.' Quietly he walked me to the bedroom door. And then he sat down at the kitchen table with a huge folio of the Talmud. He beckoned to Bubi, and the two of them began to study the Talmud in hushed tones. 'This is how I wish to part from you,' he said to my brother, 'learning a passage of the Talmud. Remember this passage when you remember me.'

I hear the murmur in the kitchen, Aunt Serena's restless tossing about on the sofa, and Mummy's quiet preparations. Outside my window the ghetto has settled down. It must be about 2 a.m.

The sound of clattering cart wheels wakes me. The house is dark. The beds and sofa are empty. Everyone is gone.

I run out of the house in my nightgown, barefoot. In the early dawn I can see the silhouette of a small crowd at the gate of the ghetto. I reach the gate, the crowd, out of breath. Mother, Aunt Serena, and Bubi are there among the handful of men and women. But Daddy is not. Daddy!

I force my way to the open gate flanked by armed military police. Daddy!

Carts are clattering in the distance. The last cart is barely visible now, but I can see Daddy's erect figure sitting among several men. His back is turned, and the outline of his head, neck, and shoulders is sharply etched into my mental vision by searing pain.

A sudden, violent shiver shakes my body. The chilly dawn is rapidly brightening into shrill morning. All at once, Mother becomes aware of my presence.

'Elli! In your nightgown! And barefoot!'

'How could you do it? You promised to wake me! How could you do this to me? I did not even say goodbye to Daddy. I could not even kiss him goodbye. How could you do this?'

My hysterical sobs surprise everyone. I am aware of the astonishment my violent display causes. But I'm powerless in the face of my savage grief. In the face of unbearable loss. I know what I wanted to tell my father in the moments of parting, and I was robbed of those moments.

All the self-delusions of the ghetto suddenly evaporate with the vanishing dawn. Oh, Daddy! How could you leave without saying goodbye? How could you leave me, Daddy?

The fathers are gone and the ghetto plunges into profound gloom. Every movement slows, every sound is muffled. Only the crying of the children is louder and more frequent. That's the only prevailing sound.

Then, another sound is added. The chanting of Psalms. The older men left behind in the ghetto now sit on the ground in the synagogue and chant the Psalms all day long. And all night long. The chanting of old men and the crying of young children blend into a slow rhythmic cacophony. The sounds reverberate in my aching belly and lull me to sleep.

The chanting goes on for six more days and nights, until it turns into a dull refrain in my soul.

CAN I KEEP MY POEMS, PLEASE?

Tables are set up in the middle of the synagogue yard. A row of Hungarian military policemen are stationed next to the tables.

In obedience of the latest order, the ghetto inhabitants stand in long lines in front of the tables, their arms laden with piles of books of every size and colour. They are delivering prayer books and Bibles, notebooks and picture albums, textbooks and novels, identity cards and passports, huge folios of the Talmud and the Torah scrolls from the synagogue.

The tables overflow with mountains of paper. The spillage of human lives, loves and identities now piled high in obscene casualness on the ground.

'This, too?' A young woman clutches a pile of family photos.

'Everything.' The Hungarian military man with a spectacular moustache is firm.

'Can I keep this one, perhaps? Just one?' The trembling hand holds the picture of a baby.

'Leave everything.'

The glossy snapshot flutters on top of the pile.

'Will we get these back? When we come back, I mean.'

'Oh, of course. You'll get them all back.'

With hesitant footsteps the young woman moves on. My brother is next in line. He dumps our books and quickly steps aside. I am carrying our documents, my parents' marriage certificate, our birth certificates and report cards, paper clippings, my father's business books, all my best notebooks saved throughout the years, and the honour scroll I had received just a few weeks ago.

There is one special notebook among them. Into this notebook I had carefully copied all my poems – one hundred and five in all. I am going to plead, politely, for my poems. I am going to smile sweetly, and ask the tough Hungarian policeman with the waxed moustache to let me keep my poems. But when I hear his rough reply to the young mother's plea for her baby's picture, when I see his face as he reassures her, I change my mind. Would we indeed get all this back? How would all this be sorted out? Even if his reassurance was sincere.

Quickly I thrust the notebook with my poems inside my blouse. With my right elbow supporting the notebook under my blouse, I hand the papers to the officer and hurry on.

My hurried footsteps carry me to our crowded little room in the far corner of the synagogue compound. I have to hide the notebook before anyone sees it. Even Mummy is not allowed to know. She would worry about the grave infraction. Quickly I tuck it deep into my knapsack all packed for departure. With suppressed excitement I run back to the yard.

I stop, paralysed. Oh, my God! Wild flames are dancing about the pile of books. A column of dark smoke is rising from the middle of the heap. They are burning our books!

I walk as if in a dream. Ash particles are flying in the hot breeze. The pungent smell of smoke fills the air. Men, women, and children crowd about the conflagration as the flames leap higher and higher, churning up blinding clouds of smoke.

The Torah scrolls! The fire is dancing a bizarre dance of death with one large scroll in the middle, twisting in an embrace of cruel passion. Aged folios of Jewish wisdom and faith tumble and explode into fiery particles, spluttering pellets of ash. Volumes of the Bible, leather-bound Psalms, phylacteries turn and twist and burst into myriad fragments of agony. Pictures and documents flutter as weightless speckles of ash, rising, fleeing the flames into nothingness.

'Almighty God, forgive our sins! Woe to the generation witnessing its Torah burnt to ashes! Woe to the generation witnessing its sacred trust trampled to the ground!'

It is the rabbi's voice. He stands with flaming eyes, tears rolling down his long brown beard. 'Woe to us, my friends, we have witnessed the burning of the Torah! Woe to us! Woe to our children! God, forgive our sins!'

The rabbi grips his overcoat and rends a tear in it. The sound of the ripping cloth jars my insides. All the men who stand near follow his example. They rend their clothes one by one, and begin the chant '*El mole rahamin . . .*' The chant for the dead.

Below my feet the flames are dancing no more. Only a huge, flat heap of grey ashes remains, a fluttery, flat heap framed by a wide edge of scorched earth. The accumulation of hundreds of lives. Mementoes of the past and affirmations of the future. My brother's tefillin, my diploma, and my honour scroll. My grandparents' picture that hung above my bed, and the novel I had been writing. My father's letters and all his Talmud. All transformed into this light fluttery grey mass.

My poems! My poems are safe. They alone escaped the fire.

Did it matter now? A stab of devastating guilt pierces my insides. Am I entitled to them?

Oh, my God, can I keep my poems?

The taste of ashes in my mouth is laced with a sudden surge of nausea. I reach the public latrine in time.

I vomit, again and again. But the taste of ashes is not extricated from my insides.

Aunt Serena

'You cannot carry all that. It's more than a hundred pounds. It'll break your back.'

Bubi overcomes Mummy's objections, and she helps him swing the loaded pack on to his back. It is a staggering load. But my prematurely tall, seven-teen-year-old brother walks with feigned ease under the prohibitive weight.

'You see? It's nothing.'

Then he helps me put the straps of my pack on my shoulders. But as soon as he heaves the pack on my back, I stagger and fall. And I am unable to regain my balance.

'I can't carry all this. I can't even stand up. How could I ever walk with this?'

'Don't be a sissy. Try.'

Mother is worried. 'No. She can't manage such a load. We'll take a few things out of the pack.'

I am embarrassed. And hurt. I so wished to carry as much as my brother. Every article of clothing, every item of food may be essential. Perhaps, pre-cisely the thing we take out of my pack will be the thing needed most. Why don't I have the courage to face carrying the burden? I hate my weakness.

Aunt Serena volunteers, 'Why don't you add those things to my pack? My pack is too light anyway. You know I can carry much more.'

But we know she can't. My favourite aunt is a gentle, frail widow in her late fifties. She has suffered from poor health most of her life. We have learned not to play rough games or make loud noises in her proximity. My kindly, soft-spoken, delicate Aunt Serena, Mummy's elder sister, has always been my special friend. Ever since I was born she has pampered me with a thousand little attentions. She would share every favourite dish, every special delicacy with me, even if I took hours to show up at her house for my daily visit.

I remembered her roast pigeon, her cocoa roll, her candied orange peel. Oranges used to be rarities in our country. One could buy oranges only in the spring, and the price would be very high. Aunt Serena would buy one orange, and wait for my visit. We would sit on the veranda, and she would peel the orange slowly, carefully separating the segments. She would hand me a segment, and take the next for herself. Each orange segment would be a tender offering of love. Each orange segment would bind us closer together.

Then she would wash and boil the orange peel in water and sugar until the syrupy liquid thickened and dried on the strips of peel, turning it into a most delectable orange candy.

'Forget it. We don't need these anyway. Forget it.'

Mummy quickly puts the things back into the cupboard. Now my pack is bearable. It still feels like a drag on my shoulders, but I manage to stand upright with it. Mother's knapsack is as large and as heavy as my brother's.

The news of liquidation had struck the ghetto like a thunderbolt. On a Thursday the Hungarian military police officer read the order. On the next Sunday, at 5 a.m., the ghetto would be liquidated. 'Every person, man, woman and child, is permitted to take along any of his personal possessions, as much as he or she can carry, but not exceeding fifty kilograms in weight. Belongings must be carried in a sack on the back. No suitcases are permitted. Be prepared to carry your load for long distances . . .'

Sunday 5 a.m.! That was less than three days away. Backpacks had to be sewn, choices made. What to cram into a pack small enough to be carried for long distances? Food? Clothing? Valuables? Where were they taking us? To a cold climate? Then warm clothes were most essential. Would they feed us on the journey? If not, food was most essential. How about gold, silver, or even china? Converted into cash, these may prove most important. Who knew? Who would guide us? I wished Daddy was here.

Mother tore up sheets and made knapsacks for each of us. My brother, Bubi, insisted on having the largest and heaviest knapsack. He wanted to carry the family burden. In Daddy's stead.

In mute stillness we moved about making preparations for departure. With averted gaze we passed each other, muffling even the sound of footsteps.

Was this the pall of defeat?

The men's chanting of the Psalms was getting louder. The young boys joined the chanters. Bubi sat among them on the floor of the synagogue. The drawn-out sound of wailing had an eerie quality in the dead silence of the ghetto. Centuries' old Jewish wailing. I hated it.

Like shadows we passed each other in the synagogue yard, not seeing. The dread knowledge of the past few days hung like a heavy veil.

A state of stupor gripped us on Saturday night, the night before departure. Mummy suggested that we test our backpacks. She thought it was a good idea to wear them for a short time around the room. Sort of a dry run. Would we be able to carry them for long distances?

Suddenly, Aunt Serena begins to scream, 'I'm not going anywhere! I'm not leaving here! I'm not going anywhere! And I will not let them have anything! Nothing! Nothing!'

She runs to the cupboard. She holds up a cup of her fine china. The cup flies and crashes against the wall. One by one, Aunt Serena smashes the entire set.

'They will not have this! And this!' Now she is holding a magnificent Dresden fruit bowl. Stunned, we watch her smash it with astonishing force against the wall. A crystal vase is now in her hand.

Mummy runs to her. She clutches her older sister in her arms. 'Please, stop. Please, Serena, stop this. Please, calm down. My darling, do not do such terrible things. Oh, no. Don't. I beg you. Everything will be all right. You'll see.'

Now I am also hugging her frantically, and I begin to sob.

'Aunt Serena, please. Come, sit down with me on the sofa.'

But she sees only Mummy. Fiercely, she turns on Mummy.

'Why do you say everything will be all right? Don't you see? They will kill us all. Every one of us. Don't you see? First they take everything from us. Then they take us far away from our home. To murder us. I am not going! Let them kill me here. And they will take nothing from me. No more!'

She grabs her pillow and in an instant tears it open. Feathers fill the room, fluttering like wild snowflakes above the debris of broken china and glass.

Bubi rushes out of the room. Mummy and I try desperately

to soothe Aunt Serena. Finally, she sits down on her bed and begins to cry softly. Mummy is crying, too. And I sob, my head buried in my pillow.

Slowly Mummy begins clearing up. Feathers, broken china, fragments of crystal. Bubi returns to the room, and we all work like robots, our limbs sluggish with dread.

Then, to sleep.

At dawn we have to be ready for deportation.

OH, GOD, I DON'T WANT TO DIE!

It is a dark, cold, cruel dawn. Mummy asks me to join her in *shaharit*, the morning prayer, and the prayer for the journey. I shiver, and pray, and gulp a glass of milk she presses into my hand. I am unable to swallow the slice of brown bread.

We join the crowd of people with bundles on their backs at the gate. I recognize the picture from a history book: It was entitled 'The Wandering Jew'. Bearded men, bedraggled women and weeping children, with bundles on their backs. I am part of that picture now. I'm one of the figures in the medieval scene. So is Mummy in her blue overcoat, hauling an outsized bundle on her back. And so is my brother in Daddy's overcoat, bent like a question mark under the weight of his enormous bundle. And Aunt Serena in her beige gabardine, huddled with her bundle like a frail bird.

A weird momentum sets the motley crowd of men, women and children into motion, and silently we march through the haze of the early dawn of the strange village. Gates open. Dogs bark. Children run into the street. Silent, furtive faces appear. Are they curious, or sad? I cannot tell. I do not turn my head. Embarrassment is controlling my movements, my thoughts.

Horse-drawn wagons are waiting for us at the end of the village. Hungarian soldiers are directing the traffic of wagons loading and departing. Dust, noise, and confusion, and the clatter of a hundred vehicles.

Bubi gets on a bright yellow buggy. Mummy, Aunt Serena, and I are directed to a drab peasant cart. A young guard from the ghetto recognizes me, and hurries over. 'Hello, Ella.'

'My name is Elli.'

'Oh, yes. Elli. Now I remember.'

Mummy and Aunt Serena take the centre seat, and I move on to a thin plank behind them. The young soldier sits next to me on the narrow seat in the back. I am embarrassed. I shoot a sideways glance at Mummy. How does she like my sitting next to a soldier? But Mummy is preoccupied with Aunt Serena who, shrunk and pale, is sunk in the depression of defeat.

The soldier wants to know how old I am, where I come from, and if I have brothers and sisters. He also wants to know what I am thinking.

'Are you afraid?' he asks.

'Yes. I am very afraid. So afraid that I stopped thinking.'

'Do you know where they're taking you?'

'I? We don't know anything. Do *you* know where they're taking us?'

No. He does not. His orders are to escort us to Dunaszerdahely, and stay there until further orders. He looks at me, and I can see sadness in his eyes.

'Do you know,' he says after a while, 'that you look very much like my sister? She has a small nose just like you, and has freckles on her nose. Just like you. But your eyes are different. She has brown eyes. Yours are blue.'

I do not correct him. The Hungarian *csárdás*, 'Blue eyes . . . Prettiest is the girl with blue eyes . . .' made blue eyes the standard of beauty. I am glad he doesn't notice that my eyes are blue-green.

During the two-hour ride, the soldier, Pista Szivos, talks about himself, his family and his expectations. He, too, loves to study. He, too, wants to get a higher education. When the war is over. On an impulse I decide to confide in him. My heart pounds with panic as I reveal the secret of my notebook with the poems. 'Would you keep it for me until the war is over?' I whisper, with suppressed excitement. 'If I return, I will look for you in your village across the Danube. If not, you can keep it.'

'You'll come back, Elli. I know you will. I will take good care of your poems. You'll get them back safe and sound. I will be waiting.'

I hope Mummy does not notice my rummaging in the knapsack. She sits gazing grimly ahead. Furtively, under cover of the knapsack's bulk, I slip the notebook into Pista's hand. Unaware, he opens it with eager interest. 'May I?' he asks.

'Oh, no! Please, don't!' I whisper in panic. 'Someone might see it.'

Uncomprehending, he looks at me. 'Why not? What's wrong?'

'The books. All books were burned. Didn't you know? I saved this from the flames. Against the order.'

In a flash he closes the notebook and puts it into his green canvas satchel. 'Don't worry, Elli Friedmann, I'll take care. No one will find out.'

I thank him and my voice quivers.

The cart now rattles on cobblestoned streets. Dunaszerdahely is packed with gawking faces. Pista Szivos grows silent, and I become aware of renewed churning in my stomach. It's almost noon.

The cart caravan comes to a halt before the town's synagogue, and we quickly disembark on to a carpet of teeming humanity. The synagogue yard is surrounded by a heavy cordon of sinister-looking soldiers in strange dark grey uniforms and black armbands.

'The SS!' Bubi exclaims with horror. 'We're being handed over to the Germans.'

'We're in God's hands,' Mummy whispers. 'Hungarians, Germans – what's the difference? God is with us. He's with us everywhere.'

I wish I felt like Mummy. To me the SS look very scary, much scarier than the Hungarians with green uniforms and expressive faces. The SS don't look human. Their faces aren't faces, they are grim masks. And their voices are angry barks.

They bark orders. We are herded into the synagogue yard jammed with men, women, children camping on the ground leaving no room to advance. As I turn back I can see our cart pull into line with the others. Pista waves goodbye and points to his breast pocket. My poems are safe. Thank you. Thank you, Pista. Forgive me. I cannot wave to signal my thanks. I am paralysed by fear.

Mummy leads the way towards the synagogue building under a shower of orders barked in choppy German. I follow, picking my way carefully so as not to step on a foot, an arm, a head sprawled on the ground.

The synagogue is brimming with a tumultuous mass of

people, baggage, prams, wheelchairs, all piled on top of each other. Excruciating noise: men, women, children, invalids — shouts, shrieks, pleas, moans, whimpers, screams, wails — and the incessant surge of newcomers. Mummy finds the staircase to the ladies' section above. Then, to the attic. Masses of people and baggage cover the stairs, the ladies' section, the attic. Mother finds an empty nook in the far corner of the attic under a dark, dusty eave, and this becomes our home for the next seven days.

Somehow news leaks out that hundreds of cattle trucks have arrived at the train station — a sure sign that our deportation is imminent. Thank God! Anything but this intolerable crowding, heat, and hopelessness.

We march again. We press on and on in the hot, hazy sunshine through the dense dustclouds whipped up by thousands of feet. At the train station, endless windowless cattle wagons, await us with doors agape in sinister silence.

Eighty-five people to a wagon. Men, women, children, infants, the elderly, the crippled. Move! Faster. *In die Waggons!* No questions, no questions. Move on, move on . . . move on!

The wagons fill fast. Those who get in first sit alongside the walls. Others crouch in the middle, feet drawn up. My brother gets a spot next to the wall. He's always the first everywhere. He offers the spot to Aunt Serena and Mummy. Bubi and I crouch at their feet. Children are held in laps. The doors slide shut plunging us into total darkness. Panic grips my bowels. I do not remember our rabbi's teaching: God is going into exile with his people. I do not sense God here in the pitch dark of the cattle truck. The train begins to move and gusts of air rush in through the gaps. A shiver runs through my body.

Oh, God, I do not want to die!

AUSCHWITZ

Some time during the fourth night, the train comes to a halt. We are awakened by the awful clatter of sliding doors being thrown open and cold air rushing into the wagon.

''Raus! Alles 'raus!'

Rough voices. A figure clad in a striped uniform. Standing in the open doorway, illuminated from behind by an eerie diffused light, the figure looks like a creature from another planet.

'Schnell! 'Raus! Alles 'raus!'

Two or three other such figures leap into the wagon and begin shoving the drowsy men, women, and children out into the cold night. A huge sign catches my eye: AUSCHWITZ.

The pain in my stomach sends a violent wave of nausea up my gullet.

The night is chilly and damp. An otherworldly glow lights up tall watchtowers, high wire fences, an endless row of cattle trucks, SS men, dogs, and a mass of people pouring out of the wagons.

''Raus! Los! 'Raus! 'Raus!'

Metal buttons glisten on SS uniforms.

'My things! I have left everything in the wagon!'

'In line! Everyone stand in line! In fives! Men over there! Women and children over here!'

Mummy and Aunt Serena and I make only three. Two more women are shoved alongside us to make it five. Bubi is shoved further, on the other side of the tracks. He turns to shout good-bye and trips on the wire fence flanking the tracks. Daddy's new grey hat rolls off his head. He reaches to pick it up. An SS man kicks him in the back, sending him tumbling on to the tracks.

Mummy gasps. Aunt Serena gives a shriek and grasps Mummy's arm. I hold my mouth: a spasm of nausea hurls vomit up my throat.

'*Marschieren! Los!*'

The column of women, infants and children begins to move. Dogs snarl, SS men scream orders, children cry, women weep goodbyes to departing men, and I struggle with my con-vulsive stomach. And I march on. Next to me Mummy silently supports Aunt Serena by the shoulder. I march and the sounds and sights of Auschwitz only dimly penetrate my conscious-ness. Daylight is skirting the clouds and it turns very, very cold. We have left our coats in the wagon. We were ordered to leave all belongings in the wagon. Everything. We would get them later, we were told. How would they find what belongs to whom? There was such wild confusion at the train. Perhaps, somehow they would sort things out. The Germans must have a system. They were famous for their order.

The marching column comes to a sudden halt. An officer in a grey SS uniform stands facing the lines. Dogs strain on leashes held by SS men flanking him on both sides. He stops each line and regroups them, sending some to his right and some to his left. Then he orders each group to march on. Fast.

I tremble as I stand before him. He looks at me with friendly eyes.

'*Goldenes Haar!*' he exclaims and takes one of my long plaits into his hand. I am not certain I heard right. Did he say 'golden hair' about my plaits?

'*Bist du Jüdin?*' Are you Jewish?

The question startles me. 'Yes, I am Jewish.'

'*Wie alt bist du?*' How old are you?

'I am thirteen.'

'You are tall for your age. Is this your mother?' He touches Mummy lightly on the shoulder. 'You go with your mother.' With his riding stick he parts Aunt Serena from Mummy's embrace and gently shoves Mummy and me to the group moving to the right.

'Go. And remember, from now on you're sixteen.'

Aunt Serena's eyes fill with terror. She runs to Mummy and grabs her arm.

'Don't leave me, Laura. Don't leave me!'

Mummy hugs her fragile older sister and turns to the SS officer, her voice a shrieking plea, 'This is my sister, *Herr Offizier*, let me go with her! She is not feeling well. She needs me.'

'You go with your daughter. She needs you more. March on! *Los!*' With an impatient move of his right hand he shoves Mummy towards me. Then he glares angrily at Aunt Serena.

'Move on! *Los!* You go that way!'

His stick points menacingly to the left.

Aunt Serena, a forlorn, slight figure against the marching multitude, the huge German shepherd dogs, the husky SS men. A savage certainty slashes my bruised insides. I give an insane shriek, 'Aunt Serena! Aunt Serena! I will never see you again!'

Wild fear floods her hazel eyes. She stretches out her arms to reach me. An SS soldier gives her a brutal thrust, hurling her into the line marching to the left. She turns again, mute dread lending her added fragility. She moves on.

I never saw Aunt Serena again.

Arbeit Macht Frei

AUSCHWITZ, 31 MAY 1944

The huge metal letters loom high and dark above the gothic gate like a sinister crown. WORK SETS YOU FREE. What does that mean? Could Mummy have been right? Could it be that we would work and be treated like human beings? Given food and proper lodgings? But free? What do they mean by that? Would they give us even freedom if we worked?

The immense portals of the gate open and we march through into an enclosure with tall wire fences. Very tall plain wire fences flanked on both sides by a lower fence of barbed wire.

It is rapidly growing lighter. And colder. Much colder. The eerie light of the watchtowers is growing dimmer. When would we get our things? I need my coat. We keep marching. On and on. Past rows of barracks, long flat buildings on both sides of the pebble-strewn road lined with barbed wire. It is a road without an end. It stretches far into the fog. And we keep marching.

Motorcycles roar past. SS officers. Dogs. Incessant barking. *'Marschieren. Marschieren! Los. Los!'*

We keep marching. On and on. It is bitter cold.

Clusters of people linger on both sides of the road,

beyond the fence. Are they men or women? Shorn heads. Grey dresses. They run to the fence and stare. Blank stares. The blank stares of the insane. They have the appearance of the mentally ill. Impersonal. This is probably an asylum for the mentally ill. Poor souls.

The road ends. Our silent, rapid, haunted march ends at the entrance of a grey, flat building. In fives we are ordered to file through the entrance. Inside, a long narrow room, very low ceiling. Inside, shocking noise. Shouts, screams. Loud unintelligible screams.

'Ruhe!' Quiet!

A tall husky blonde in SS uniform shouts, 'Ruuheee! Wer versteht Deutsch? Deutsch! Wer versteht Deutsch, 'raustreten!' Who understands German? Step forward!

I step forward. I understand German. A few other girls also step forward. They probably also understand German.

'Tell them,' the big SS woman roars. She tosses a chair towards me. 'Stand on this and tell them to keep quiet at once. I want quiet this minute. Next minute they will be shot!'

I attempt to shout above the din. And other interpreters, they too shout as loudly as they can. The low ceiling compresses the sound. The noise is like a roaring tidal wave hurling back and forth. Stunning us senseless.

'RUHE!' The buxom SS woman leans forward and cracks her whip into the crowd. As if on cue, the SS soldiers lining the walls step forward and begin cracking their whips, snapping into faces. A sharp pain slashes my left cheekbone. I feel a firm welt rise across my face. Why? I am the interpreter. Quickly, I step down and melt into the crowd. Perhaps it is safer there.

Within seconds it becomes quiet.

'*Auskleiden! Alles herunter!*' Everyone undress! Everything off! '*Los!*'

The room is swarming with SS men. Get undressed? Right here? In front of the men? No one moves.

'Didn't you hear? Take off your clothes. All your clothes!'

I feel the slap of the whip on my shoulders and meet a young SS soldier's glaring eyes. 'Hurry! Strip fast. You'll be shot. In five minutes anyone with clothes on will be shot!'

I look at Mummy. She nods. 'Let's get undressed.' I stare directly ahead as I take off my clothes. I am afraid. By not look-ing at anyone I hope no one will see me. I have never seen my mother in the nude. How awful it must be for her. I hesitate before removing my bra. My breasts are two growing buds, taut and sensitive. I can't have anyone see them. I decide to leave my bra on.

Just then a shot rings out. The charge is ear-shattering. Several women begin to scream. Others weep. I quickly take my bra off.

It is chilly and frightening. Clothes lie in mounds on the cement floor. We are herded, over a thousand shivering, humiliated, nude bodies, into the next hall, even chillier, darker. Even barer and more foreboding.

'*Los! Schneller, blöde Lumpen!*' Move. Faster, idiotic whores.

We are lined up, and several young women in grey dresses start shaving our hair – on our heads, under our arms and in the pubic area. My long, thick plaits remain attached while the shaving machine shears my scalp. The pain of the heavy plait tugging mercilessly at the yet unshaven roots brings tears to my eyes. I whisper a silent prayer for the shaving to be done quickly. For this unexpected torture to be over soon.

As my blonde tresses lie on the ground, the husky, indifferent hair butcher remarks, 'A heap of gold.' With a shudder I remember the scene at the selection – the SS officer admiring my '*goldenes Haar*', the separation from Aunt Serena. Where was she now? Was her hair shorn off as well? Did she also have to strip naked? Was she very frightened? Poor darling Aunt Serena. Where was she now? Had my hair been shorn off before the selection we would be together with her now. We would not have been separated. It was because of my blonde plaits that Mummy and I were sent to the other side. Poor darling. If only we could have stayed together!

The shaving of hair has a startling effect. The absence of hair transforms individual women into like bodies. Indistinguishable. Age melts away. Other personal differences melt away. Facial expressions disappear. In their place, a blank, senseless stare emerges on the thousand faces of one naked, unappealing body. In a matter of minutes even the physical aspect of our numbers seems reduced – there is less of a substance to our dimensions. We become a monolithic mass. Inconsequential.

The shaving of hair has another curious effect. A burden is lifted. The burden of individuality. The burden of associations. Of identity. The burden of the recent past. Girls who had continually wept since the separation from parents, sisters and brothers, now keep giggling at their friends' strange appearances – shorn heads, nude bodies, faceless faces. Some shriek with laughter. Others begin calling out names of friends to see if they can recognize them now. When response comes from completely transformed bodies, recognition is loud, hysterical. Embraces are wild, noisy. Disbelief is shrieked, screamed, gesticulated. Some girls bury their faces in their palms and roll on the ground, howling.

'*Was ist los?*' What's the matter? A few cracks of the SS whip, and order is restored.

I look for Mummy. I find her easily. The hair cropping has not changed her for me. I have been used to seeing her in her kerchiefs, every bit of hair carefully tucked away. Avoiding a glance at her body, I marvel at the beauty of her face. With all accessories gone, her perfect features are even more striking. Her high forehead, large blue eyes, classic nose, shapely lips, and elegant cheekbones are more evident than ever.

She does not recognize me as I stand before her. Then, a sudden smile of recognition: 'Elli! It's you! You look just like Bubi. Strange, I've never seen the resemblance before. What a boyish face! They cut off your beautiful plaits . . .'

'It's nothing. Hair can grow.'

'With God's help.'

We are herded *en masse* into the next hall. I shriek with sudden shock as a cold torrent of water gushes unexpectedly from openings in the ceiling. The mass of wet, nude bodies crushes about me in a mad, splattering wave. In a few minutes it is over and I am carried along in the midst of the wet mass to another hall. Grey, sack-like dresses are shoved at us and we are ordered with shouts of '*Los, blöde Schweine*' to pull them over wet, shivering bodies. The epithet '*blöde Lumpen*', idiotic whores, is now downgraded to '*blöde Schweine*', idiotic swine. More despicable. And it is upgraded only occasionally to '*blöde Hunde*', idiotic dogs. Easier to handle. Everyone has to pick a pair of shoes from an enormous shoe pile. '*Los! Los!*' Take a pair. Size makes no difference.

As we emerge from the other end of the building and line up quickly in rows of five, shivering wet in shapeless grey sacks, with heads cleanshaven, the idea strikes me. The strange creatures we saw as we entered the camp, the shaven, grey-cloaked bunch who ran to the barbed-wire fence to stare at us, we are them! We look exactly like them. Same bodies, same dresses, same blank stares. They, too, must have arrived from home recently. They, too, were ripe women and young girls, bewildered and bruised. They, too, longed for dignity and compassion. And they, too, were transformed into figures of contempt instead.

The *Zählappell* lasts almost three hours. This word, meaning roll call, becomes the dread and the lifestyle of Auschwitz. Twice daily we are lined up in fives to be counted. At 3 a.m. we would line up with lightning speed, and then stand stiffly and silently for three or four hours until the official SS staff shows up to count our heads. The SS officer taps the heads of the first line and counts in multiples of five. The actual count is accomplished in a few minutes. The stiff, silent wait on the evening *Zählappell* lasts from five to nine. The line-up has to be mustered in seconds in order to stand for hours, waiting.

It is inconceivable to me that the mad rush inside would culminate in an interminable wait outside. Why are our wet, traumatized bodies, wearing only a single cotton cloak, hurled out into the cold for an endless, senseless wait?

Finally, a smartly stepping, brisk German military staff member appears. With the tap of an authoritarian stick on the shaven head of the first girl in every row of five, we are initiated into the camp. We have become members of an exclusive club. Inmates of Auschwitz.

BORN IN THE SHOWERS

AUSCHWITZ, 31 MAY 1944

Newborn creatures, we marched out of the showers. Shorn and stripped, showered and uniformed, we marched. Women and girls from sixteen to forty-five, rent from mothers and fathers, brothers and sisters, sons and daughters and husbands – transformed into a mass of bodies, we marched toward the barracks of Auschwitz.

An abyss separated us from the past. The rapid succession of events this morning was an evolution of aeons. Our parents and families belonged to the prehistoric past. Our clothes, our shoes, our hair – had they been real? The homes we left only recently were in distant lands, perhaps of make-believe.

We were new creatures. Marching expertly in fives at a rapid, deliberate rhythm, we were an army of robots animated by the hysterics of survival.

We survived the entry into Auschwitz. Unknowingly, we survived the selection of the diabolical Dr Mengele, the handsome psychotic monster who had tenderly stroked my 'golden hair' and in a kindly voice advised me to double-cross his SS machinery and lie about my age to save my life.

As we march in a deliberate, rhythmic, robotlike

manner towards our future in Auschwitz, a heavy cloud of smoke rises from the stacks of low, grey buildings on our left. It was only much later that we found out about the smoke. By then we knew all the faces of death. By then we had lived long enough in the realm of death to believe what we found out about the smoke.

But now, as we march from the showers towards the camps, we know only of survival. We sense its sinister significance. Survival is programmed in every fibre of our muscles, and with those muscles we march, not understanding, not even wishing. We march on, driven by instinct. We march, steadfastly avoiding German whips, growling German shepherds, and poised German guns. With inexorable drive we march silently on and on. That quality, born in the showers, that new, mystical compromise with death, bids us to move on. Our secret pact with death animates our march towards the camps.

When we reach C-Lager, the sun is high. It scorches my freshly shaven scalp. It parches my lips and throat. My shoes, two sizes too small, are pressing on skinned toes and ankles. My own mystic march against death is turning into a graceless limp. Relentless heat, suffocating dust, and the monotonous drone of marching feet. Thirst. Unbearable. God, let me faint.

It is Sunday. We have not had anything to drink since Thursday morning. I had wet my lips in the shower, but the whole thing was too sudden and ended too abruptly. I had had no chance to drink. Now I am unbearably parched. The sun is blinding. As I touch my smooth scalp it burns my palm. Gun butts glare. A motorcycle whizzes by soundlessly, as if in a dream. What a sparkling sight! Everything is flooded with brilliance, even the white, brilliantly white, rising dust. Oh, God. Is this a dream? A nightmare?

The camp is a huge barren enclosure fenced in by barbed wire. Half-built barracks stud the horizon. Deep craters block our advance towards the barracks, and we are ordered to reroute our path around them.

'Zählappell!' With automatic speed we line up in fives in front of a flat, narrow brick building under construction. No windows or doors. This is our block. The entire camp is under construction. Was there water in the block? No, there was no water in the block. There is no water in the entire camp.

After Zählappell we are permitted to disperse. News of our arrival has spread like wildfire. Large numbers of young women swarm about us. A mass of faces. A rising tide of clamour – shrieks, shouts, savage exclamations. What are they shouting? What is all the mad excitement about?

They are all inmates of this camp, brought here weeks ago. All are anxious to meet relatives. Their eagerness is like a mad hunger ready to attack us, to devour us with a passion like the scorching sun. I have not fainted yet. I am standing in the midst of this blinding mad place, in the midst of the blinding sun, the white-hot rising dust, the wild clamour. Yet I have not fainted. I am standing barefoot, my ankles and toes bleeding, on scorching ground. I need water.

From the sea of random din, words precipitate and float towards me: 'Where are you from? What city? What town? Which ghetto? Do you know if Budapest has been liquidated? How about Komárom? How about Dés? Miskolc? Have you heard of Kisvárda? Of Debrecen? Of Szeged? Have you? Have you?'

'Is there water in this camp? Please. No, I haven't heard anything about Budapest. I don't know if Komárom has been liquidated. No, I don't know of Kisvárda. Or Debrecen . . . Where is water?'

'Where are you from? Which ghetto? Tell us. Tell us, please.'

'Is there water in your camp? We are from Somorja. Slovakia. Upper Hungary. We don't know anything about anybody. We have been on the road for over three days, and before that under guard in the ghetto, over a month. We have no information about other places. We arrived this morning. The men were taken away. The elderly. And the children with their mothers . . . to the other side. That's all we know. Where can I get a drink of water?'

The crowd keeps growing. New faces, eager, expectant faces.

'Somorja? Upper Hungary? Then you know Guta. Do you know the Weiss family from Guta? The Rosenbaums from Galánta? Do you know the Guttmanns from Surány? Did you see them?'

'Bubi!'

The maddening heat. The crowd. The thirst . . . My God, am I going insane?

'Bubi!' No, no. I refuse to go mad.

A pair of brown eyes is peering into my face. 'It's Elli! Look, Hindi, it's Elli. Elli's here! Oh, Ellike!' She holds me tight. 'I thought you were Bubi. You look just like him.'

'But who are you?'

'Don't you recognize me? I'm Suri. Suri Schreiber, your cousin.'

'Suri!' I scream. 'And you're Hindi. My God, you are here, too! When did you get here?'

'We came a few days ago. Who is with you?'

'Mummy. She is with me here. But everybody else was taken away. Daddy, Bubi, Aunt Serena. I don't know where they are.'

'Only young women and girls are here. We were also separated from everybody. Mummy, Father, Layi, Breindi, Aunt Chaye and Grandmother went to the other side.'

'What about Benzu? And Elyu?'

'Benzu was taken to the Russian front several months ago. And Elyu is in a Hungarian labour camp. Only the two of us remained. But now we found you. We will be together from now on. Where is Aunt Laura? Let's go look for her.'

Suri and Hindi are my cousins from Sátoraljaujhely, in Hungary, daughters of my father's sister, Aunt Perl. Four years ago I spent part of my summer vacation in their house. The happiest vacation of my life. It was a large house with many children and cats. Hindi was the eldest, about nineteen. Suri was sixteen, a brunette beauty. Layi was my age, and Breindi a year younger. The two boys, Benzu and Elyu, treated me like an equal although they were much older than I. Benzu was twenty-one and Elyu seventeen. Benzu, the handsome ladies' man, and Elyu, the yeshiva student with black hat, long *peyes*, and large blue eyes. My grandmother, ignoring her lame leg, lorded it over the roost. Aunt Perl, a heavy-set, good-natured blonde whose laughter rang like bells throughout the house, and Uncle Abram, a Hasid with a rich brown beard and generous disposition, looked to Grandmother for advice and discipline. She held the reins of family and business.

Now they all were gone. To the 'other side'. Only Suri and Hindi are here.

We go to look for Mummy and find her lying on the ground. She is half asleep, her lips cracked. A red blister has formed on her nose, covering its whole length.

Mummy is surprised to see my cousins but too exhausted to exhibit joy. Her first question is, 'Where do we get drinking water, do you know?'

There is no water in this camp, Hindi and Suri explain. There is black coffee in the morning and soup in the evening. During the day the inmates drink from the lake.

'Lake? Where is it?'

Mummy wants to go to the lake at once. Suri and Hindi lead us to a puddle, a large hollow in the ground filled with murky water. It has an unpleasant odour.

'To drink from this? It's putrefied! It's filthy! It stinks!' I look at my cousins with horror. 'You drank from this?'

'We all did. There is nothing else. If you are thirsty enough you don't care.'

I am thirsty enough. My tongue is covered with a layer of whitish stuff, and my lips have begun to crack. But I could never drink from the filthy, smelly swamp!

Mummy bends down and takes a handful of water to her mouth.

'It's not so bad. Hold your nose, then gulp. It's not that bad. Drink, Elli. I feel a little better already.'

I raise a palmful of swampy water to my lips. The smell makes my stomach heave. But I have no urge to vomit. My stomach has been empty for a long time.

I close my eyes and hold my nose with my other hand. Then I quickly slurp. It is not bad at all. As a matter of fact, I like it. I delight in the touch of wetness on my lips, mouth, throat. I take another palmful and drink, now greedily gulping without holding my nose. The smell does not matter. The water quenches and revives.

'No more, Elli. Please, don't drink more. Some girls got very sick. They drank too much.' Hindi forces me to spill the third palmful.

The women in our transport are sprawling on the ground when we get back from the 'lake'. Most are lying with eyes closed, oblivious to the bustle around them. The shouting and calling of names continues. Sudden exclamations of recognition, frantic embraces, shrieks, cries, more embraces. Some lonely figures move on, looking and searching further, appearing more forlorn and dejected with every failure.

With every 'Don't know' answer, I feel the weight of their search. And it drones on, the continuous confrontation with young girls searching for families, friends, security of contact. Every 'Don't know' brings visible despair. I start to modify my style: 'The transport you're looking for is over there. Perhaps they know . . .'

Mummy has long withdrawn from the crowd. Overcome by fatigue, she sits in one of the deep holes.

Suddenly I spot a tall figure wandering about, shouting, 'Laura! Laura! Laura!'

'Aunt Celia!'

It is Mummy's sister, my youngest aunt. My beautiful, stylish aunt. Even now, as she meanders about in the drab grey garb with shaven scalp, she looks distinguished.

'Aunt Celia!' The vehemence of my embrace almost sweeps her off balance. She grips my shoulders and stares into my face. Her eyes open wide with shock and disbelief.

'Elli! My little Elli! Is it you? Here? There are no children on this side. How is it possible? Oh, my God! Oh . . . my darling.'

She rocks me in a tight embrace. She is kissing my scalp. And we both begin to weep.

'You're here. My little darling . . . Are you alone?'

'Mummy is here, too. Come, I'll take you to Mummy.'

'Your Mummy is here, too? My God, my God . . .'

We find Mummy sleeping in her hole. Aunt Celia kneels and strokes her face. Mummy opens her eyes wearily, as if in a drunken haze. Then suddenly she recognizes her sister's tear-stained face, and she sits up in alarm. 'Celia!'

Aunt Celia crawls into the dusty hole and the two sisters hold each other in a silent clasp. They have not seen each other for three years. And now, a reunion in the scorching hole, in Auschwitz.

Still sobbing, Aunt Celia reaches into her bosom and takes out a lump of black substance tied on a string around her neck. She unties it and hands it to Mummy. 'Here. Eat it.'

'What's this?'

'It's bread. My bread. My bread ration. Eat it. It's yours. I want you to have it. You must be very hungry.'

'This is bread? It looks like a cake of mud. How can you eat this?'

'Eat it. You won't get anything to eat until the evening *Zählappell*.'

Mummy takes a bite and tears spring into her eyes. 'I can't eat this.'

'You must. There's nothing else.'

She takes another bite, swallows it, and promptly throws up. Her tears flow on dusty cheeks. 'I can't. I'd rather starve.'

Aunt Celia cries, too. She bends down to wipe away the tears with the edge of her prison garb. 'Laurie, if you don't eat you will not live. You must.'

I snatch the bread from Mummy's hand and begin to eat. The dry, mudlike lump turns into wet sand particles in my mouth. The others have eaten it. I swallow. The first food in Auschwitz. To survive.

Aunt Celia tells us her husband and son have been arrested by the Arrowcross, the Hungarian Nazis. My cousin Imre is seventeen, tall, dark and very handsome, a virtual copy of Aunt Celia.

We decide to form a family of five and vow never to be separated from each other.

Suri says it is much easier to survive in Auschwitz if you are five. Bread and food is distributed at *Zählappell*. Every five get one portion of bread and one bowl of food. Those ahead of you take the first bits of bread and the first gulps of food. If you are tall and stand last, you get the smallest piece of bread and the bowl may be empty by the time it reaches you. But if you have family or friends in the line, you are careful to share it equally.

We stand together at evening *Zählappell*. But when the bowl of food is handed to me, I am unable to take a gulp. It is a dark green, thick mass in a battered washbowl crusted with dirt. No spoons. You tilt the bowl until the mass slides to the edge, then gulp. The dark mush smells and looks repulsive. The edge of the bowl is rusty and cracked and uneven with dried-on filth. My nausea returns in a flash. I quickly hand the bowl to Mummy. She takes a gulp and begins retching. I try again. This time I take a mouthful but cannot swallow it. It has grains of sand in it, just like the bread, and something else — pieces of glass . . . and wood . . . and cloth. I spit it out and begin to vomit. My empty stomach feels as if it were rising through my gullet.

'Never mind. We all threw up at first. But then we learned to swallow it. It's food. You must eat to live. Close your eyes. Hold your nose. Now, gulp.' Suri's gentle but firm admonition gives me impetus. I gulp. And again. Four times.

'Good girl.' What wisdom moved my beautiful sixteen-year-old cousin to store in a few days the secret of survival against all odds? The secret of triumph over death? And what cruel fate ultimately robs her of it? I never find out.

Our family of five is separated during *Zählappell*. Aunt Celia, Hindi and Suri are ordered back into their blocks.

Mummy and I stand on *Zählappell* until long after nightfall. It turns very cold. Under the loose garb, the chill wind reaches every particle of my bare body. A slow shiver begins on the lines. In time, the rhythmic shiver of thousands standing on *Zählappell* in the dark, cold nights of Auschwitz will become a familiar sound. But now it is new to my ears. It is the conclusion of my first day in Auschwitz. The first day of my new life.

THE RIOT

AUSCHWITZ, 31 MAY 1944

The riot occurred during the first night in Auschwitz.

There were no beds in our block. Each group of five received two army blankets. One for mattress, the other for cover. The unusual hardness of the floor, the close proximity of strange bodies, and extreme exhaustion after the long, traumatic day made sleep impossible. The windows had no panes. Cold wind penetrated the blanket. There were muffled cries in the dark. Slowly, finally, I drifted off to sleep.

A shriek tears into the night. In seconds the block is agog with screams. A wave of panic sweeps the prone bodies, whipping them into wild frenzy. Shrieking senselessly, girls begin trampling upon each other in the dark.

'I smell gas!' someone shouts. 'They are exterminating us!'

Many surge for the door. It is locked. They begin pounding on it. A shot is heard outside. Then a second, followed by a barrage of fire. The screaming stops instantly. The door is thrown open. German guards are shouting orders: 'Back on the floor! Lie down and don't move! Or you'll be shot!'

There is dead silence. Suddenly a girl screams, 'Mummy! Mummy! They are killing my mother!'

Another shot rings out.

'*Ruhe*. Quiet. Or you'll be shot.'

But her shrieks grow more frantic. 'Mum*myyy*! Where are you? Mum*myyy* . . . They are killing my mother! Everybody, listen. Hear the shots? Oh, Mummy. Oh, God, they are killing her!'

The silhouette of a body sitting upright is outlined in the middle of the room. Someone places an arm around her shoulders, trying to soothe her: 'Shush. Quiet. You had a nightmare. Lie down here, next to me. Lie down. Here.' The hand gently draws her down on the blanket, but the body jerks away, springs up and begins to scream again, a bloodcurdling scream: 'Let me go! Let me go to my mother!'

The door opens, and two German guards enter, their guns drawn. 'Who is shouting?'

Flashlights train on the lone standing figure.

'*Komm mit.*' Come along. '*Los!*' Each guard holds on to an arm, and the young girl, still screaming, is led outside. Seconds later, a shot rings out.

I sit up with alarm. 'They shot her?'

'Shush, please. For God's sake, quiet, everybody. We don't want another riot. It's dangerous.' It is the voice of the gentle woman who had tried to quiet the hapless young girl.

At dawn we're aroused for *Zählappell*. It is still totally dark when we line up. The sky is studded with stars. It is cold. Some girls bring their blankets along and the whole row of five stands wrapped in one blanket. Why didn't we think of that? But soon a gruff girl appears and orders them to return the blankets. As the girls obey and run towards the block, the young woman in charge lands a heavy blow on the head of each with her enormous stick. She is our *Blockälteste*, the head of our block.

She had been brought to Auschwitz with a transport of sixteen-year-old girls from Slovakia in 1942. Two years in Auschwitz! Survival at incredible cost. She is eighteen now, thin but strong, her face set in a countenance of grim determination. Or defiance. And anger. It is a face of unapproachability. *Blockälteste* are the absolute commanders of the block. They have private rooms in the block and supervise their charges at all times. But in our block there is no extra room, or any facilities, so our *Blockälteste* sleeps in another block. But she knows of the riot.

'You are lucky you were not all shot for what happened in your block last night.' Her tone is as cold and hard as ice. 'Sabotage! Do you know the meaning of sabotage? If it happens again, you will be sent to the gas. The entire block. I am responsible for your conduct. If any of you makes sabotage at any time, I shall report you immediately. This is your warning.'

Gas? What gas? What did she mean, 'You'll be sent to the gas?' Could any of those horrible rumours actually be true? What was sabotage? She did not explain, and no one asked questions. And no one asked who the young girl was whose broken heart had set off the riot. No one mentioned her name. Where was she from? She was a dark, nameless silhouette in the night, and like a shadow she disappeared in the night. Only her shriek remained. We all carried her shriek in our souls.

Teen Vanity

Today, the fourth day in Auschwitz, I saw myself for the first time. As we were approaching the last block on our way to the latrine, our guard stopped to chat with another guard. While we stood patiently waiting, I glanced at the window nearby and saw my reflection in the glass pane. I did not recognize myself. I was a shocking sight.

The latrine is a long, wide ditch where we are taken under guard in groups of fifty. Luckily, the German guards cannot bear the stench and stand at a distance while we use the ditch. This makes the latrine an ideal place for meeting friends and relatives. Here we resolved to meet Suri, Hindi and Aunt Celia at noon. We have no watches and cannot tell time. Noon we can tell by the sun.

At first I panicked at the latrine. The ditch is very wide and very deep, and I had nightmares of falling into it. Mummy was holding me by the hands while I crouched above the smelly abyss, and I held hers while she did. But after the first few times I learned to balance at the precarious edge, and now the fear is gone. Amazing how fast one learns. Everything. Even swallowing the dark, daily mush became easy.

Lying on the hard floor is also easier now. And the *Zählappell* is quite bearable.

We are aroused at dawn, and it is totally dark when we line up for *Zählappell*. Gradually it grows lighter. The stars fade and a cold gust buffets my bare body under the thin dress. I crouch, hugging my knees in order to keep warmer and control my fierce trembling. Mummy promises to poke me when someone approaches so that I can quickly stand upright.

All at once I notice that blood is flowing on the legs of the girl before me. Oh, my God, she must've been shot! I panic: What should I do? Then in a flash I realize: She is menstruating. We have no underwear, no sanitary napkins . . . the blood simply flows down her legs. Poor girl. My God, this is horrible. Why doesn't she say something? Ask for a rag, or something? Whom can she say anything to? From whom can she ask for anything? She might even get shot for bleeding. Does menstruation constitute sabotage?

How lucky for me that my last menstruation was just over when we arrived. I'd rather die than have blood flow down my legs! In full view. Oh, my God! I could not bear it. But . . . what about next time, in less than three weeks? There'll not be a next time. By then the war will be over, and we'll be free. This cannot last much longer. It's impossible to survive this much longer.

Getting used to thirst is the hardest. I'm always thirsty. For Mummy hunger is hardest. She complains of being hungry all the time. But for me, thirst is much worse. The only fluid we get is four gulps of a black liquid called coffee at the morning *Zählappell*. I think I'm going mad with craving for water all day long. We are forbidden to leave the area of our block, so the 'lake' is out of bounds. No drinking all day and all night.

The sun is scorching, and we loiter aimlessly about the block all day. We are forbidden to enter it during the day, or sit in its shade. But sometimes we take a chance and sit, even lie, on the ground behind it. When a German approaches we give a slight kick to girls who have fallen asleep, and in a flash they are on their feet. Mummy keeps falling asleep, and I keep guard. When it's her turn to keep guard, she also falls asleep. It is better that I lean against the wall of the block and sleep that way. I can keep alert when I sleep standing up.

From the scorching sun our faces blister and crack. Brownish discharge oozes from the cracks and forms large crusts around the edges. Our faces look ridiculous and repulsive.

I definitely look more ridiculous than most girls. My extremely fair complexion responded to the fierce sun by sprouting large blisters ringed with red on my nose, my cheekbones and the back of my neck. My ears look enormous because of towering blisters on my earlobes. I look like a clown. A mass of pus sores around my cracked lips makes me look as if I'm wearing a perpetual grin stretching to my ears.

My hair has started to grow on a scalp flaming red from the onslaught of the sun. The sharp, yellow bristles against a scarlet backdrop make my head look like a blushing porcupine.

During the night of the riot someone had torn my left sleeve at the shoulder. Now the sleeve hangs folded to my elbow. On the exposed shoulder another blister has popped up.

I walk barefoot since I cannot wear the shoes I received in the showers. They are too small. Huge, silly blisters also cover my feet. A large blister blew up on the side of my right leg. Someone had kicked me in the cattle truck and the bruise, after festering for a while, also turned into a huge, domelike blister.

So, my ludicrous looks are compounded by a strange limp. With blisters also on my soles, I have not managed to devise a graceful manner to navigate. How can Mummy and my cousins claim that I look like my brother Bubi? He is handsome with perfect features. And I? My God! I am a disfigured scarecrow.

How is Bubi now? Is my handsome brother also disfigured by sun and thirst?

THE DAWN OF NEW HOPE

It's our tenth day in Auschwitz. Today Aunt Celia is going to join us, right after *Zählappell*. Last night she sneaked into our block with the happy news that a woman in our block was willing to change places with her. From now on we will stand *Zählappell* together. Suri and Hindi are also looking for girls willing to change places with them. Then we will be a row of five together. There is a much better chance to make it when you are five together. You share the soup equally. You warn each other. You help prop each other up during the long stand. I can't wait for this *Zählappell* to be over.

Here they come, marching smartly, a delegation of five SS officers. Rapidly they count the heads of the first row. All's in order. Then they bark an order. What was it? March?

March! The first rows begin to move, and we follow. We are marching past the row of blocks towards the gate of the camp. The gate opens and we march through. We are marching on the gravel road between two rows of barbed-wire fence, past rows and rows of blocks. 'Look, Mummy. We are leaving the camp. We are leaving Auschwitz!' But

Mummy does not relax. She is worried about leaving her sister behind.

'We had no chance to let Celia know. Or Suri and Hindi,' Mummy whispers. 'What will happen to her, my poor little sister? She has had diarrhoea for three days now . . .'

We were told that diarrhoea was very dangerous in Auschwitz.

Our march leads to the showers. With practised speed we undress. The stares of the SS guards no longer matter. We feel no nakedness without our prison uniforms as we felt no clothedness in them. Our bodies have lost dimension. It is our souls that are naked, exposed, violated.

The shower and shaving are by now familiar experiences. And so is the wet, shivery wait on the outside – the *Zählappell*.

We are ordered to march. Again we pass many camps beyond barbed-wire fences lined with gawking inmates, tall watchtowers, and finally, the high, forbidding iron gate crowned by the huge, black, spidery letters – ARBEIT MACHT FREI!

We are leaving Auschwitz!

The station comes into view. A long row of cattle trucks. Barking dogs. Barking SS guards. Familiarity breeds less fear.

I have a pair of shoes now. They fit, and give me a new outlook on life. As the train begins to move out of Auschwitz's morning fog, I feel curiously elated.

'Mummy, you'll see. We're going to a better place. You'll see. Let's thank God that we've left Auschwitz behind.'

Mummy is silent. The ordeal of separation from her sister is a heavy burden. The train rolls amid stark hills, forlorn farms. The cracks of the wagon afford a view. At times we stand still for hours. At dusk we roll into a dense forest, and the train comes to a halt. We spend the night standing still in the depth of the forest. When light begins to sift through the cracks of the wagon, the train begins to move again.

The wagon is not jam-packed this time: we even have room to lie down. Five sisters with lovely voices lead us in singing familiar tunes, and soon the memory of Auschwitz dissipates in the dawn of new hope. I join in by reciting poetry, and many of the girls respond in a chorus to the refrain of my most popular poem, 'God, Help Our Beloved Nation . . .'

The train slows to a halt at a station. The sign reads KRAKOW. I remember learning about Krakow in school. It's the capital of a province of Poland called Galicia. My father's family originated from Galicia. In Krakow there is a large and prominent Jewish community. Or, rather, was. All the Jews must have been deported from here long ago.

''Raus! Alles 'raus. Aussteigen!' Out! Everybody out! Off the train! We are driven in open army trucks through a cold, dismal, rainy morning, across winding, hilly roads. The sky is heavily overcast. Large drops of rain hang on a huge sign in German and Polish above a wide metal gate: CAMP PLASZOW.

The gates open, and we roll into a circular clearing surrounded by high hills. Rows of barrack-blocks are neatly set about a central square with a high flagpole flying the SS flag. Here the trucks discharge their cargo of one thousand women with their freshly shaven heads glistening against the darkened sky.

We have arrived in Plaszow, the most notorious forced-labour camp in Poland.

'Mummy, There's a
Worm in Your Soup!'

PLASZOW, JUNE 1944

The brief morning *Zählappell* is followed by a work
line-up of thousands of inmates. The dreaded *Kapos*
arrive, and each *Kapo* selects several hundred workers
for his brigade from among us.

The word *Kapo* means supreme authority over life
and death. Delegated absolute power by the SS, the
Kapos of Plaszow, as if they had made a pact with the
devil, exercise all methods of control – brutal beat-
ings and torture to death – with relish. They seem to
rise above the need for human response, or contact,
even among each other.

I observe with dread the awesome figure of our
Kapo standing high on a rock or boulder, whip in
hand. Several younger assistants snap to his command. If you stop to rest for a moment, the *Kapo*
instantly dispatches one of his boys and the lash
whips you back to your routine. Were the lad's blows
tempered with a touch of compassion, the *Kapo*
would admonish from his high perch: 'At her head,
Liebling! Are you losing your touch? Let her have it
in the head!'

If you cried out in pain, the lashings would dou-
ble. In time we learned to stifle even our whimpers.

In time we learned to endure in silence.

Our work consists of *Planierung*, straightening the hilltop with spades and shovels in preparation for construction. The work was very difficult in the beginning. When we first arrived in the hills, we were exhausted from the mountain climbing alone. And that, at the start of a twelve-hour workday.

Now that we've become somewhat acclimatized, the work is much more bearable. The bruises on our hands have turned into callouses. Our backs are used to bending without pain. Digging, shovelling and wheelbarrowing have become endurable. If only we could stop to rest for a few moments from time to time!

Yesterday an older woman a few feet from me stopped to rest her arms. Instead of taking the trouble to administer the whip, the young assistant picked up a piece of rock and slung it at her. It slashed a deep, bloody gape in her head, and she collapsed unconscious. The boy, taken aback, ran over to the stricken inmate, then turned apologetically to his master. The *Kapo* admonished with a devilish chuckle, 'You missed, you stupid *Junge!* She's only fainted. You should've struck her dead!'

At noon we have half an hour's rest when we receive our cooked meal. It's a bowlful of porridge, or cabbage soup with grain.

This morning the food arrived early. As it stood for hours in the sun, it became putrefied and alive with worms. I noticed a long, white worm wiggling in Mummy's spoon as she lifted it to her mouth. I shrieked with horror. Mummy was startled; she looked at me with astonishment. 'What's wrong?'

'Mummy, there's a worm on your spoon! Look, Mummy, there are hundreds of worms in your bowl! And in mine! Look!'

'Nonsense! These are not worms. Eat, and leave me alone.'

'But, Mummy, these are worms. Live worms. They crawl. Look.'

I pick one of the swarming creatures out of my bowl and place it on the ground. It begins crawling. Then I pick another. It, too, begins crawling.

Mummy looks at me with helpless despair. 'What are you trying to do? What is your objective? Tell me, what do you want of me?'

I do not understand. I wanted to save Mummy from a horrible fate: disease, or death. Or simply from the horror of swallowing worms. Instead, she is furious with me. My mother – the finicky lady who had been reluctant to eat in restaurants, and even in friends' houses, for fear the vegetables, or hands, were not washed thoroughly enough, who baked not only cookies and cakes but even our daily bread at home, for fear the flour in bakery goods had not been carefully sifted – now is glaring at me.

'I can't leave this food. I am very hungry. Do you want me to die of hunger?' Her voice is beyond recognition. Her facial expression is beyond recognition as she goes on, 'And there are no worms in it! Say no more of it!'

As Mummy continues eating I turn my bowl over, spilling its contents on the ground, and run. I sit on a boulder at a distance, and begin to cry. My God. My dear God, is this actually happening?

ALIEN HEROES

One hot day in July, about three weeks after our arrival, our lunch is interrupted by an unusual sight. We are working in the *Planierungs* Brigade that day, digging and levelling the hilltop right above the camp. We are sitting on the slope and eating our soup directly overlooking the camp's main square, when large covered vans appear.

Men and women in civilian clothes descend from the vans, and are roughly herded into the SS command block. The civilians are well dressed and have an air of independence about them. Like people. Not like camp inmates.

One of the men makes a defiant gesture as an SS man jostles him forward with the point of his gun. The civilian, a tall man in a grey trench-coat, turns and jostles the German. A shot is heard and the civilian in the trench-coat collapses. Then he stands up and starts to run. Another shot. The civilian tumbles. A third shot levels him prone on the ground. The civilian begins to crawl, drawing a line of red in the dust. The German soldier goes wild. He discharges a barrage of bullets into the crawling figure, then starts kicking him uncontrollably. All the other civilians are jostled and shoved at gunpoint until they disappear behind the door of the SS command block. The single figure in the grey trench-coat remains lying in the dust in the centre of the square, a pool of blood ever widening about him.

We go on eating our soup. There is no time to pause: this is Jacko's brigade, the *Kapo* under whom there is no talking, no stopping for rest, and barely enough time to finish your soup.

The windows of our block face the windows of the SS command block, and in the evening we can see the interrogation. The civilians are brought into the room of the commandant one by one, and questioned. They are severely beaten in the course of questioning. The shouts of the SS and the shrieks of pain keep us awake all night long.

At the morning *Zählappell* in the main square I chance a surreptitious glance towards the flagpole, where the civilians, about sixty people, are lined up. This morning they look more like rag dolls than people. They are haggard, dishevelled, and stand in a scraggly formation like doomed souls. The only human emotion visibly animating them is fear.

From time to time I watch them as I work from our site on the mountain. I see them being marched to a block off the square. What will they do to them?

Then about ten people are marched out into the square, and lined up against the centre wall opposite the flagpole.

One SS man does the shooting. Like target practice, he fells the civilians, one by one.

The next row of ten is shot by another SS soldier. Against the same wall the next ten are lined up. In order to reach the wall they are obliged to step over the bodies of the first ten victims. I see a young woman, also in a grey trench-coat, fall on the body of a man she is about to step over, and remain lying draped over the body until a German soldier hauls her to her feet and thrusts her against the wall. He shoots her along with the others.

Row after row, the firing squad concludes its task and marches off. The bloodied bodies remain scattered about the square. Suddenly, one body, that of a man, begins to crawl in the direction of the departing Germans. One of the German soldiers notices him, and turns. At that moment, the condemned victim hurls himself on the soldier and tackles him to the ground. The other soldiers rush to their comrade's aid and free him from the grip of his profusely bleeding attacker. The wounded civilian is finally felled by bullets discharged from three German guns simultaneously.

The indifference of my fellow inmates is shattered for the rest of the afternoon. At the risk of grave punishment, we keep glancing down at the prone bodies in the central square of the camp below us.

This was my first direct encounter with death. Or was it? What we had just witnessed, and its aftermath – dead bodies strewn in the dust, grey, indifferent, coloured by pools of blood – was this death? Or was it something else, something much more inexplicable?

Towards the evening, as we approach the camp, my throat tightens. I am apprehensive about having to pass the blood-soaked bodies on our way to *Zählappell*. Will there be a smell? I have heard that corpses decompose fast in the heat. These corpses have lain in the sun all day.

To my great relief, by the time we reach the camp the corpses have been cleared away. The square is empty except for the large pools of blood. After *Zählappell* we are ordered to carry pails of water from the well beyond the last block and wash and sweep away the blood.

Touching the blood with my broom creates a curious bond with the fallen victims. Grief, compassion and fear – successfully repressed on the mountain – now well up in an overwhelming tide. I can barely control my nausea.

Who were they, these men and women in elegant trenchcoats with dignity intact? Who were they and what had they done to be crushed so ruthlessly, so cruelly? What did their last defiant gesture mean?

Oh, how I hurt for them. How I hurt for these alien heroes. For the futility of their heroism. How I hurt for the futility of it all.

What is death all about? What is life all about?

THE UPRISING

PLASZOW, JULY 1944

In mid-July a diarrhoea epidemic sweeps the whole camp. In a few days it reduces us to raglike dolls barely able to walk. I am dizzy, and Mummy keeps encouraging me to breathe deeply and walk erect. I have violent abdominal cramps. The pain is unbearable. The routine continues, however. *Zählappell*, march to work, twelve-hour workday. On the verge of collapse, we carry on.

Until one day. It is a cold, rainy day, and by early afternoon we are drenched to the bone, digging the heavy, soggy ground with heavy, wet shovels. A sudden downpour sends us scampering for cover under nearby huts on stilts. While we huddle under the dripping planks, a team of SS officers headed by Camp Commandant Goetz arrives to survey our work. Their indignation fills the air with shrill tones and the barking of dogs. The *Kapo*'s henchmen wield whips under the huts, and in moments we are back on the job. Shivering miserably, we fail to comprehend. We have committed sabotage. Sabotage witnessed by Commandant Goetz and his staff!

At the evening *Zählappell* the dreaded news is

announced. At dawn, we will be decimated, the punishment for sabotage.

We have heard of decimation. Our fellow inmates from Poland mention the word frequently enough. In earlier years, the entire camp, or a block, or a work brigade, would be decimated for every minor infraction. The inmates of the guilty unit would be lined up at dawn, face a firing squad, and every tenth by an SS officer's count would be shot. No one ever knew where the count would start and who the tenth would be until the moment the shot rang out. One, two, three, four, five, six, seven, eight, nine, and . . . ten . . . Shoot! Sometimes they would start counting in the middle of the row. Sometimes at one end, then switch directions. You never knew if you would be tenth. Not until the last moment.

Now it is our turn. Our brigade would be lined up at dawn and . . . It cannot be true!

'It's true all right,' said Felicia. 'You've committed sabotage. SABOTAGE! For sabotage they usually shoot the entire brigade. You got off easy. Only decimation.'

Decimation, my God. I may be the tenth. Or Mummy. My God, what if it's Mummy?!

I am unable to swallow even a spoonful of the evening soup. For the past several days I have not eaten more than a spoonful or two. The diarrhoea has depleted my appetite. I have been constantly thirsty. Now I cannot swallow at all. Mummy keeps pleading, 'Eat. You won't be able to go on if you don't eat.'

Go on? We are to be decimated at dawn. One of us will surely turn out to be the tenth . . . Go on? Where? If Mummy dies, I die. Oh, God, let me be the tenth!

I weep hysterically. When I have to go to the latrine, I insist that Mummy come with me, and when she has to go, I insist on going with her, so that we should be together every moment of the night. Every moment left to us. We spend the night holding each other in the bed or walking to the latrine. The diarrhoea epidemic is still going strong.

This is a new experience in terror. I am terrified of dying. I am apprehensive of the sensation of the bullet penetrating my body. Of my blood flowing. I keep seeing my bullet-ridden body in the dust, my blood colouring red the grey dust of the square . . . Yet I am even more terrified of seeing my mother shot. The thought of her falling into a red pool of blood convulses my insides. I have a steady pounding in my temples. A sense of strangulation in my throat, my chest. A slow pain creeping upward from my bowels.

There is a soft murmur from the bed above. The girls from Guta are reciting the Psalms. The chant of the doomed. They have a small prayer book from somewhere, and have managed to hide it. They say evening prayers daily. Sometimes they lend the prayer book to Mummy and she also says the prayers.

Mummy whispers to them, 'Please, say it a little louder. So we can follow along.'

The murmur is louder now. Mummy and I are able to repeat the verses in Hebrew after them. The pounding in my temples subsides.

In a pause between passages I can hear muffled sobs. Almost all our block belongs to the *Planierungs* Brigade and is involved in the sabotage. Soon we realize that the entire block is awake. One by one, all the girls join in reciting the Psalms. The sobbing grows silent.

Furtively I keep glancing at the window. It is still dark. Thank God.

The first feeble shafts of dawn begin filtering into the

block. The reading stops abruptly. A hush stifles even our breathing.

'Read on,' someone calls. 'Read on until they come for us.' And the two little skinny sisters from Guta read on while the light turns brighter and brighter. The chill morning breeze sends shivers through the bunk beds. The reading of Psalms emanates through chattering teeth.

It is bright morning now, and no one comes for us. What time can it be? They must have decided to shoot us at the regular *Zählappell*.

'It's six thirty. Time for *Zählappell*,' calls Felicia the *Blockälteste*. But her voice is not savage. It is tired and sad. She must know something. No one dares to ask questions.

Slowly, heavily, we file out of the block.

The morning glare is blinding. A strange brightness envelops the blocks, the square. I tremble with the terror the cool breeze stirs on my skin. We huddle, Mother and I, in an embrace of rhythmic shivers on *Zählappell*. Soon the SS will arrive.

The sun rises and the glare becomes unbearable. We stand for over two hours, our trembling numbed into a faint echo. I am very tired.

The SS do not come. All the camp stands wearily for hours, and the SS do not come. Felicia bites her lip nervously. What happened? The *Lagerälteste*, the head of the camp, a tall, thirty-ish prisoner with the immobile face of an Indian chief, keeps walking away from his post near the flagpole. What is going on? The tension is unbearable.

Then, all at once, the *Kapos* come. Hurriedly, each selects his brigade. Our *Kapo*, Jacko, detaches his brigade without a word, and with a jerk of his head indicates that we follow him.

Follow him, just like that. Just like every other morning. Simply march in formation behind Jacko, out of the square, through the gates, in the direction of the mountain. Away from camp. Up the mountain, to the spot where we interrupted our *Planierung* yesterday. Yesterday. Only yesterday I held this shovel. It is still wet. The ground is still soggy from yesterday's rain. Only yesterday.

Just another day of work begins. No one speaks. We are alive. Alive. The sun is shining and the wet grass is brilliant green. The sky is azure. A soft, soft breeze. My tiredness turns into drowsy fatigue. In a dreamlike trance I dig into the soft earth. It is July 1944, and I am alive. Thirteen and a half, and alive. It is a clear, beautiful day.

What was happening? Why didn't they shoot us? Had they postponed it until tomorrow?

The conversation starts slowly. Most of the girls are of the opinion that the decimation will take place tonight or tomorrow morning. Some even know of other instances, in the earlier days, when such things did take place. Quite often. The Germans would do this in order to torture the condemned inmates. They would do this daily for a week sometimes. Every evening the decimation would be announced for the following dawn, then postponed, unannounced, for another day.

But I stop worrying. I am basking in a miracle. I had known with all my heart that Mummy or I would be dead today at dawn. I had felt the pain of the entering bullet, had tasted the blood. I had seen my bloody corpse strewn in the dust among the others. I had experienced death. And now I am alive. I have seen the sun rise. I am touching the earth, the grass. I am here on the mountain. It is so simple, to be alive. You move, you breathe, you touch. You feel the air about you. You can see, see far about you. The mountain, the people, the blocks. The sky. I stop being afraid.

There is feverish activity down below. Large trucks are rolling into the camp. The trucks discharge a great number of civilians. There are hundreds in the square and the SS surrounds them with guns drawn. They are taken into the command block, a few at a time, then hustled back into the trucks and driven away. More trucks come, with more prisoners. Some in dark-green overalls, or are they uniforms? In handcuffs. All are taken into the command block, then driven away in the trucks. This goes on all day.

Back in camp, we are totally ignored by the SS. The roll call is done by the *Lagerälteste*. After *Zählappell* we are herded into our block and told to stay indoors.

From our windows we can see trucks with prisoners coming and going all night long. We can hear prisoners being interrogated in the command block.

The next day all is quiet again. All is routine. The decimation is never mentioned again. Apparently more important events replaced it on the SS agenda. Rumours had it that an entire factory had staged an uprising, management and workers, and the SS was busy with that. Others said the green-uniformed prisoners were partisans, underground fighters, from the hills, and now an offensive was being mounted against them.

Soon more rumours circulate about the partisans. It is believed that they came into the nearby hills in order to stage an attack on our camp and free the inmates. The attempt was unsuccessful, however. It was discovered just before the actual assault, and now the Germans are cracking down on the whole countryside. Some inside contacts were discovered in the camp, and now these contacts are being used to track down partisans in the hills.

What if the partisan liberation attempt had worked? The night we spent in terror of death by decimation would have been the night of our delivery. Just like the story of Purim. But it failed, and we continue as slaves of Germany.

Yet, a miracle did occur. The episode of the factory uprising or partisan attack discovered during the pre-dawn hours of our scheduled decimation saved our lives.

Hitler Is Not Dead

**PLASZOW, 20 JULY – AUSCHWITZ, 8 AUGUST
1944**

A shocking sight on the square – the flag with the brilliant red swastika is flying at half-mast. At *Zählappell* a whisper reverberates through the ranks.

'Hitler is dead!'

More rumours: Russian troops are rapidly advancing. Unrest in Berlin. Unrest in German ranks on all fronts. Things are converging towards the end.

On a scorching August morning, trucks pull into the camp square, and we are loaded on to them. The endless caravan of trucks pulls out of the square, out of the camp. The entire camp is evacuated.

The trucks bounce through winding roads among the familiar hills. Where are we going? The station of Krakow comes into view. It, too, is familiar. We saw this station seven and a half weeks ago, when we arrived. Only seven and a half weeks ago. Yet long, long ago. Before I became part of death and blood and naked horror. Before I experienced decimation, tasted death itself. It was before I saw people tortured and shot. It was before I knew that there were no limits to human cruelty.

In these seven and a half weeks I have changed. I have grown into a concentration-camp inmate. I have learned to live with fear and hunger and abuse. I have learned to swallow dirt and live worms. I have learned to endure cold, pain and long hours of hard physical labour. I have learned to live with waning hope and cling to reality born of pretences. I have learned to wait . . . and wait . . . and wait.

I have become very thin and very tall. My neck is long. My hair has grown, and now it stands erect, about an inch high, like a crown of yellow bristles about my head. Other girls have boyish hairdos. Some have curls framing their faces. But I have a crown of thorns like a porcupine. My cheekbones protrude so sharply that sun blisters have formed on each because of their extreme exposure to the sun. Sun blisters have blown my lips up like those of a clown.

The sun is blazing as we inundate the train station, a weary human overlay covering the platform and the field far beyond. Hours pass under the glaring sun. At long last the loading into wagons begins.

'One hundred to a wagon!' the *Kapo* snarls.

One hundred, my God! There will be no room even to sit. I hope at least one of us will get sitting space. Mummy is fading, overcome by heat. She must have space to sit.

We are shoved and pushed into the wagons. Mummy gets a spot near the wall and I sit on her legs. But soon she is compelled to draw up her legs tightly to her as more and more people are pressed into the wagon and complain that she is taking up too much room with her legs partially stretched out. She starts to explain that I am sitting on her legs, saving space. She is kicked and told to draw up her legs. I stand up, and she draws up her legs. I am unable to stay on my feet. I am pushed and shoved and keep falling on top of others sitting. Mummy screams, 'Leave her alone!' She tries to get up and give me her place but as she scrambles to her feet, others press into her place, and she tumbles.

More and more people are pressed into the wagon. The heat and stench keep increasing. Air is steadily drained from the wagon. Breathing is becoming difficult.

The train stands for hours. More trucks arrive. Dogs bark. Shouts. And more shouts. Then we hear a *Kapo*: 'Thirty more in every wagon!'

Thirty more? That's impossible. We are on the verge of passing out. The crowding, the heat, and the lack of air are beyond endurance. Thirty more and we will suffocate.

The inmates from Poland, the old-timers, assure us that it is possible. There have been precedents. Incidents in which more than half of the transport suffocated before they arrived at their destination.

Soon we discover that it is possible to absorb thirty more. Noise subsides as the sweating bodies are pressed closer together. Breathing is difficult. No one speaks. The lack of air imposes its own dominion. You simply comply. Sit or stand with your mouth open, eyes half closed. Do not breathe but draw in air in short gasps. Do not sit or stand upright but lean against the body next to you. Let your body go limp. Do not think. Let your mind go limp.

Mummy is sweating profusely. She is unable to wipe her brow: someone is sitting on her shoulder. I keep mopping her face with the hem of my uniform. She closes her eyes. She falls asleep, I think. But then with alarm I realize she has fainted. What should I do? Many others faint. They are white, with their eyes closed and their mouths wide open. They are piled one on top of the other in silent heaps. The woman Mummy is lying on has fainted also, patiently tolerating Mummy's inert body on top of her. Earlier she grumbled every time Mummy moved, poking her with a knee or elbow. Now both are still. Their breathing is laboured, plaintive.

As the evening bears down, the heat grows more oppressive. Loud wheezing and hoarse moaning break the density of the darkness. By now I am lying drenched in sweat on a pile of bodies. Someone is lying on top of me, lifeless, wet and heavy. I cannot move. I do not know where Mummy is. She must be nearby. Perhaps in the same pile. I do not know.

Some time during the night the train starts to move. The rattling of the rapidly moving train drowns out the sound of moaning, and I feel better. The movement of the train, the sensation of going ahead, inspires confidence. There is life in movement. Hope. Standing still is terrifying.

The train moves all night and all day. The second night we reach an area where the air is somewhat cooler. We must be travelling north. Breathing is somewhat easier. The moving train sucks in air through cracks in the wagon wall. Most people revive.

Mummy also revives. She insists that I sit in her place while she stands up. But she is unable to. I stand and crouch alternately throughout the day and the night that follow.

On the morning of the third day the train comes to a halt. The doors open and chill air rushes into the wagon. Dazed by the light and air, we scramble slowly to our feet. Some are unable to get up. I have to pull Mummy to her feet.

Men in striped uniforms drag us like rag dolls off the train. For over two days we've had no body space, no food, no water to drink, and very little air to breathe. Our limbs are cramped, our lungs and brains are compressed. The freedom of space and movement is now overwhelming.

As I stagger out of the wagon, my glance falls upon the sign of the station: AUSCHWITZ.

So Hitler is not dead, after all.

TATTOO

The motorcycle stirs up dust as it roars past us. Mummy has barely enough stamina to straggle along. The train ride from Krakow has drained her of energy. And of determination. She has lost her will to live. As we stagger into marching formation on the Auschwitz platform, she seems unable to grasp the mechanics of survival. She wants to stay in the wagon with those unable to walk. She is indifferent to the implication of this. She just insists that she is unable to march, and pleads with me to leave her behind.

In my alarm, I grab her arm and shake her violently. 'Stop that! Do not say that! You can walk. Come. Walk!'

I pull and drag her along. Like a puppet on a string, she starts to move her legs involuntarily and keep pace. When the selection officer appears on his motorcycle alongside our rows on the road to camp, and asks straggling women whether they could work, Mummy whispers to me, 'I cannot work. I cannot even walk. I will not even reach the camp.'

'Yes, you can walk. In camp we will get food. And water. And you will feel better,' I hiss between my teeth.

Now the motorcycle is coming back again. It comes to a sudden halt. The tall, heavy-set SS officer in grey uniform approaches our row. My throat tightens. My heart pounds so loud I am certain he can hear it. God, let him pass us! Let him drive on! God, save us! But I can feel his gaze. We march on, stoically dragging our feet in a desperate effort at speed, not even glancing in his direction. His scrutinizing stare pierces my awareness. He keeps pace with our row. Our row. There is no mistake about it. He is watching someone in our row!

Suddenly, his stick reaches into the middle of our row. His stick taps Mummy on the shoulder. 'Hey, Grandma, can you still work?' To my astonishment, he speaks Hungarian. A *Volksdeutsche* from Hungary! An ethnic German from Hungary; a volunteer in the SS army. They were worse than the Germans.

Mummy crashes on, ignoring the question. As her silence confirms his suspicion, the SS officer is about to reach for her arm and pull her out of the marching column. I poke her sharply in the rib and whisper under my breath, 'Say yes. Say it, for God's sake!'

She turns to the SS officer. Her voice is the thin, high-pitched screech of a bird, barely audible. 'If I must, I will. I will work.'

For one awful moment time stands still. Then the officer swings back on his motorcycle and drives on. My legs tremble. Thank God. My dear God!

Mummy marches on like an automaton.

When we reach camp, we are handed slips of paper. A number is written on every slip. We are lined up to have the numbers tattooed on our arms.

The lines are long. The sun burns the top of my head. Through veils of fatigue persistent thirst penetrates. But

Mummy bears it silently. Indifferently.

I notice the tattoos on one line are smaller and neater than the rest, and once again I drag Mummy to the end of that line, a much longer one. Poor Mummy. Poor, poor Mummy.

We languish hour after hour on that line. Finally, Mummy's turn comes. I support her while she holds her emaciated arm for tattooing, and while the number A-17360 is tattooed slowly, neatly, painfully on my arm.

During *Zählappell* there is a sudden downpour. We stick our tongues out and turn our open mouths to the sky. Rain drops on dry tongues, flows into parched throats. Wet, cold, wonderful raindrops. We suck in drops from our lips, hands, and arms. It rains and rains, and we lap insatiably.

Mummy is somewhat revived. She no longer needs my support but stands on her own, and, raising her face to the heavens, allows the cold rain to run over her closed eyes and perfectly sculpted cheeks. Rivulets of rain run from her cropped head down the high cheekbones, along her swanlike neck to the sloping, bony shoulders. How beautiful she is!

A new dimension has been added to our identity. A number freshly tattooed on our left arms. I am no longer anonymous. I have a name. It is A-17360.

The Broken Bed

AUSCHWITZ, 8 AUGUST 1944

It is nightfall when, wet and chilled to the bone, we are herded into a cell block. These barracks are different. They are unlike the partially constructed ones in the previous camp in Auschwitz or the ones in Plaszow. Is Aunt Celia still there in that camp? And Hindi and Suri? Will we ever meet them?

These blocks are huge, elongated, brick buildings with enormous portals on each end. When you enter, you are overwhelmed by the building's size, its height and length, by the endless rows of bunk beds reaching to the ceiling on either side. A forbidding gabled roof looms darkly above. A curious, chest-high, brick structure runs down the middle, slicing the block lengthwise into two equal halves. A dank, dark dread hangs in the air.

The beds consist of wooden planks, forming even squares covered with army blankets. We are permitted to get on the beds, twelve women to each square. The tiers are so low that when I'm sitting upright my head touches the tier above.

I take off my soggy dress and crawl on the lowest tier next to Mummy. I am glad to get under the army blanket on the bare wooden planks. It stills my shivering somewhat. Ignoring the din about her, Mummy is lying with eyes closed, motionless.

There is a sudden sound of crashing from above. One of the planks in the tier above cracks, sending the women on the plank into shrieking laughter. Mummy, directly below the dangling plank, is oblivious to what is happening. All other women on our level move to the side. Only Mummy remains, lying motionless, inches below the broken plank.

I attempt to rouse her, but she refuses to move. In a frenzy, I step up on the ledge to speak to the women above. I plead with them to get off the plank so as not to break it completely. But they laugh at my alarm. Food distribution is in progress, and each is eagerly awaiting her turn. Not one of them pays attention to my frantic pleas.

I have no other choice but ask the *Blockälteste* to help. She is a robust, pretty brunette from Slovakia who addressed us in flawless Hungarian when we came into the block. We found out her name was Elsa Friedmann, and that she was sixteen, the daughter of a shoemaker from Presov. I am going to explain to her that I do not wish to get the women into trouble. I only wish the *Blockälteste* to order them off the tier until it is repaired. I am sure Elsa will understand that, and not punish them for having refused my request to move.

I find Elsa at the entrance to her room. She is giving orders to her aide about the distribution of the food. As neither of them pays attention to me, I apologize to Elsa, and explain that my request is extremely urgent. Elsa glares at me. 'Go back to your place immediately!'

'Please, understand. The bed is broken above my mother and she is too weak to move away. Please, tell the women to get off the cracked plank before it breaks completely and falls on my mother. Please. They will listen to you . . .'

My voice chokes with anxiety. Elsa looks at me incredulously. 'You! You dare come here and interrupt. Get out of here, you stupid little dog!'

Her outrage is underlined by a fierce blow to my right cheekbone. My head reels from the impact of the slap. My eyes fill with tears. I run back to the bunk. The plank is dangling precariously and the women sitting on it are unconcerned, absorbed in their food. Perhaps I am wrong, after all. Perhaps the plank is not going to break. Perhaps it is all sheer hysteria on my part. I am too young and too scared and excessively concerned about my mother because I am still a child. The grown-ups know better. I thought I had grown and matured in the camp, but I still behave like a baby.

I am hurt and very tired. I lie down next to Mummy, determined to stop worrying about the broken plank. After all, if it breaks, the women above are liable to get hurt, too, and they do not seem worried. Why am I alone such a coward?

The food is now being distributed to our tier. I manage to raise Mummy to a sitting position and place the full bowl in her lap. She begins to eat. But when I reach for my portion, the cauldron is empty. I have to wait for the next batch. I lie down again, supporting Mummy's back with one hand.

There is a sudden loud bang. The entire upper bunk comes crashing down. I am aware of a sharp pain on my forehead: a plank has pinned me to the bed. There is broken wood all about me. Women are screaming. Naked bodies are dangling in the thick dustcloud.

Slowly I move my head to the right to see if Mummy is all right. I cannot see anything as another broken plank presses against my right cheek, blocking my view. But I hear a thin, high wail from the other side of the plank. And again: 'Yaaaaay . . . yaaaay . . .'

It sounds as if it is coming from very far away. Yet I can hear it amid the noise. All at once I realize it is my mother's voice. Right next to me. My God, she must be badly hurt.

I start to move my shoulders and realize that I am completely free, except for my forehead. Pressing against the plank with one hand, I manage to free my head also. Sliding on my back, I start to crawl out from under the debris.

I see Mummy pinned under a huge pile of wood in a most peculiar position. She is lying on her back but her head is bent forward in such a way that her face stares at me in a vertical pose. It is terrifying. Her eyes are wide open but she does not seem to see me. She keeps emitting that eerie, high-pitched wail: 'Yaaay . . . yaaaay . . .'

The women are still sitting on top of the broken planks, some shrieking in pain. I begin to yell hysterically, 'Get off! Get off this instant! There's someone right underneath you. You're crushing her to death!' Like madwomen, they keep on screaming and crying, ignoring my shouts. I begin pulling them by their arms, savagely pummelling those who pull back. I cry and yell and pound at their naked flesh.

'Ellike, what's the matter?' It is Mrs Grünwald, a neighbour from home. 'What happened?'

I am unable to speak. I point at Mummy's body under the rubble. Mrs Grünwald shouts at the women, and several of them get off the bed. Others refuse. They are simply beyond caring.

With the help of Mrs Grünwald and her daughter Ilse, I lift the plank that presses Mummy's head against her chest, and start to pull her out by the legs.

'Leave that white thing alone, and help me!' Mummy cries. 'What's that white thing you're pulling there?'

I am in shock. 'Mummy, it's your leg. I'm pulling you out by your leg. Mummy, don't you feel it?' Mummy does not answer. She closes her eyes. The three of us manage to pull her out from under the debris and place her on top of the brick divider. She falls into a stupor. She does not respond to my voice, or to my touch.

A young fellow inmate, a doctor, tells me to find a sharp object, a pin, for instance. Someone hands me a needle, and the doctor pricks Mummy in several places. Mummy does not respond. The doctor's face is grim as she pokes the soles of Mummy's feet with the needle, and the lifeless body does not stir.

She puts her arm about my shoulders. 'You're a big girl now. You'll understand. There's no sensation in your mother's body. She's unconscious, and totally paralysed. I think her spinal column is broken. She'll never regain consciousness. It's a matter of hours. You must be prepared. You must brace yourself.'

No! No! No! This cannot be. I will not live if Mummy dies.

IS IT TRUE ABOUT THE SMOKE?

AUSCHWITZ, AUGUST 1944

I am sitting on top of the brick structure at Mummy's head. A steady stream of rain pours on her head from a leak in the roof directly above, and I keep wiping the rainwater off, all night long.

It's very cold in the cell block. I am wet, and chilled to the bone. And very hungry. Because of the accident, I did not receive my bowl of food in the evening.

Mummy must be cold, too. Her feet feel like ice. But I have nothing to cover her with. I can rub her legs with my hands to warm them. I rub Mummy's legs and wipe the rainwater off her face in turns. From time to time, I bend over her mouth and touch her lips with my cheek. She's breathing. Thank God.

At dawn I can see that Mummy's eyes are partially open. At times they flutter wide open, and stay open for several seconds. Please, please, let her live. I implore you . . . Let her live. If she will not, I will die, too. I cannot go on without her . . .

I must leave Mummy and line up for *Zählappell*. The *Blockälteste* informs me that Mummy cannot stay in the cell block: I must remove her to the *Revier*. The *Revier* is the infirmary. Here the sick and the invalid are held for up to a month. Once every month there is a selection at the *Revier*, and those who have not recovered are removed.

Mrs Grünwald and Yitu Singer, our rabbi's daughter from Somorja, help me carry Mummy to the *Revier* on a stretcher.

I'm not permitted to visit Mummy at the infirmary, but Juliska, our doctor from home, brings me daily reports about her condition. But that is only in the evening, and I'm anxious about Mummy all day. Every morning after *Zählappell* I sneak to the end of the row of cell blocks, to the last one, which holds the infirmary, and hang around there. Whenever one of the staff comes out, I inquire about Mummy. Some stop and respond. Others just glare and say nothing. I then rap lightly on the wooden wall and call Mummy's name in hopes of finding her.

Once a patient answers and says that Mummy's bed is further on, and that Mummy is alive. Thank God.

Soon I find the exact spot where Mummy's bed is standing. Rapping on the wall and repeatedly calling to her, I hope to raise Mummy from her stupor and stimulate her to speak. All of a sudden I notice a loose knot in the wooden wall. As I am poking it, the knot gives way and falls in. I peek inside and can see the top of Mummy's head quite nearby.

'Mummy,' I call in ecstasy. 'Mummy, I can see your head!'

Mummy answers! Her voice is tired but distinct. Her words, slow, halting, form a question: 'Ellikém . . . My little . . . Elli. How are you?'

I cannot answer. Tears choke me. This is Mummy as I know her. She has recovered her speech. She has recovered her old self.

Daily I linger near the infirmary waiting for the right

moment to sneak to the knothole and speak to Mummy. One morning she tells me she can lift her head. The next day Mummy can lift her right arm. Then she begins to sit up in bed. And then she starts to complain of hunger. Thank you, my God. Mummy is getting better. Mummy's going to make it.

Most of the time I have to hide behind the *Revier* so as not to be discovered by the SS. Sometimes I can speak only a few words to Mummy. If I notice a guard approaching, I disappear like lightning. But those few words sustain me for the rest of the day.

One morning, as I am talking to Mummy through the knothole, an SS guard grabs me by the shoulder, and marches me to the command block. This is it. This is the end. How will I be executed? Will they shoot me? Send me to the gas chamber?

I am not shot. I receive a punishment. I am ordered to kneel on the gravel in front of the command block for twenty-four hours without food or drink.

The command block is far from the cell blocks, right at the entrance of the camp. The carpet of sharp, black grit upon which I have to kneel stretches to the barbed-wire fence. I have to kneel facing the fence.

Beyond the fence I can see a road flanked on the far end by barbed wire, and beyond that fence, endless rows of cell blocks identical to the ones in our camp. From the spot where I kneel, I can look down the road in both directions and see infinite rows of cell blocks like ours, covering miles and miles . . . as far as the eyes can see.

The immense proportion of Auschwitz strikes me for the first time. Never before had I had the chance to see this. A world of barracks and barbed wire.

The road is busy with constant traffic. Trucks and various

military vehicles rush past. Clusters of people keep marching by, men in striped uniform accompanied by SS guards and dogs. Women drawing carts with huge cauldrons, others carrying huge cauldrons on thick wooden bars across their shoulders. Women and men in varying degrees of malnutrition.

There are some who can barely walk, and it seems they are going to collapse at any moment. Others seem like darkened skeletons, yet they walk upright, without faltering. No one looks to the side. Not one of them takes notice of me. They move as if animated by a magnet pulling them into one direction, straight ahead.

Suddenly, a marching column appears. Men and women and – children! They are marching in rows of five. Women with hair, wearing colourful clothes, some with hats on. Men and young boys and little children! A little girl is clutching a doll. Their faces are white, without blisters and sores. They walk fast, breathless, afraid. But they walk like people, nervous and alert. They are not robots animated by an unseen external force. They are people, moved by a force within.

They must have just arrived in Auschwitz! From the outside. They still wear the expression of the free. They have not yet acquired the posture of the inmate. How different they are!

Some people glance at the barbed wire in my direction. Several women look at me curiously. A young woman even smiles at me. I take a rash chance, and call out to her, in German.

'Where are you from?'

'From Lodz.'

'Did you say Lodz?'

'Yes. The Lodz ghetto.'

'You came now from Lodz?'

'Yes. We've just arrived.'

Her last words reach me from a distance. She is marching on with the transport at a fast pace. A little boy has just dropped his clown. As he is about to pick it up, a motorcycle approaches. An older boy who holds the little boy's other hand gives him a tug, and the little boy marches on without his clown. The clown, dirty yellow, remains at the roadside.

The columns march on and on. Row after row after row. Then they are gone. All's quiet, and the dust settles. Then traffic resumes. But the clown lies still in the sunshine.

My dear God. The little children. The little girl with the doll. The little boy without his clown. And all the others. The little children of our transport, three months ago. A lifetime ago. Where are they all? Where did they march? Where are these men, women, and children marching? From where I kneel I can see the smoke, not too far away. I have seen it all morning. I have smelt it all night. Dear God. Have mercy.

The older inmates have told us that our camp was adjacent to the crematorium, and the smoke smarting our eyes, our throats, our lungs is the smoke of burning bodies.

Is it true, dear God? Is it true that the little children are trampled underfoot in the gas chamber? Is it true that the stronger adults struggle like wild animals to reach pockets of air high up and trample the weaker ones and the little children?!

They told us, over and over again. So we should stop screaming when we heard it. So we should believe it.

I'm getting dizzy from the heat. The sun is high and strikes my bare scalp with relentless fury. I am very thirsty. The sun's glare is blinding. My throat is dry. The sun . . . I can't bear the sun.

My dear God. Have mercy.

The Selection

AUSCHWITZ, AUGUST 1944

'I'm asking you to risk your life,' I whisper. 'I need your help.' Without a moment's hesitation Mrs Grünwald's reply comes, 'I'll come.'

'I'll come, too,' young Ilse Grünwald volunteers.

'God bless you,' I whisper. 'I'll be back.'

I need one more person to help me sneak Mummy out of the infirmary and carry her all the way to our cell block. It is a dangerous undertaking – and if we get caught we will be sent to the gas chamber. I had been warned by the SS commandant that I would be put to death in the gas chamber if I as much as approached the vicinity of the *Revier*.

But I have no alternative. Mummy must be smuggled out. Dr Tauber, our young doctor friend from Somorja, had sent me an urgent message: 'The selection is scheduled for tomorrow morning. All the sick in the *Revier* beyond three weeks will be taken to the gas chamber. Your mother is unable to walk or stand for longer than a few seconds without support, and she has been hospitalized for three weeks. If you want to save her life, you must get her out of here immediately. . . .'

I must act at once. I need one more person. In the

dark cell block I find Yitu's bed and climb to the second tier. She is not asleep. She nods. Yes, she understands the plan. Yes, she's willing to join us. I can barely fall asleep. Please, God, help us.

At dawn Mrs Grünwald, Ilse, and Yitu join me near the entrance of the block, and the four of us walk casually towards the infirmary. We pray silently as we slither through the semi-darkness. No SS guard is in sight. It's forbidden to walk unescorted even to the latrine. We have to wait for at least fifty girls to gather and then request an SS guard to escort us on the short distance to the latrine. Sometimes it takes hours for an SS guard to appear. We learned to wait, and control nature. No one would dare to leave the confines of the block unsupervised.

And now we are walking alone, the four of us, without permission, without an escort, to the vicinity of the infirmary, an area strictly out of bounds. God help us.

Still there's no SS in sight. We make it to the infirmary. As soon as we reach it, I quickly rap on the wall, and within an instant, four nurses carry Mummy through the door. Only two of us can carry her at a time. We chain-link our hands, and the nurses place Mummy on our locked hands in a sitting position. Mummy is able to lock her arms about our necks, and in this fashion we carry her a few steps. Then the other two take over. None of us is strong enough to carry her longer than a few steps. Walking as fast as we can, we reach our block undetected. Thank God.

The inmates are lined up for *Zählappell*. We sneak among the lines one by one. Mrs Grünwald and I carry Mummy behind the lines, and place her on the ground in a crouching position. We cover her with our bodies until the SS arrive for the roll call. But Mummy is unable to crouch long. She can only lie, or sit propped up against my legs with her feet stretched out. We have no choice. We must take a chance and let Mummy sit in a propped-up position. When the SS man approaches, several girls help me pull Mummy up on her feet. I stand behind her, my body giving her support. And so she stands for the few moments it takes for the SS to count the heads of the first row nearby.

It works. Thank God. But how long can this be kept up? Two days? Three days? And what then?

Mummy cannot walk to the block after *Zählappell*. She has to be carried. The *Blockälteste* must not notice. If she sees her, she will report her as an invalid. She will not take any chances of harbouring an invalid in the block. That is unquestionable sabotage.

We succeed in smuggling Mummy into the block and hiding her in the bunk. The day passes without incident. But what will I do tomorrow? Will my friends come and help me carry Mummy unnoticed to the *Zählappell* again? Will they stand by me, risking detection every moment?

There is a sudden commotion at the front end of the block. It must be near midnight, the lights have long been out. What is all the noise about? The news spreads rapidly. Selection. Tomorrow at dawn, the entire block will stand for selection. Women from our block will be selected for work in factories in Germany.

Selection! How will Mummy pass selection? I have just smuggled her out of the *Revier* to avoid selection, to save her from the gas chamber. And now . . . Oh my God, what have I done?

THE TRANSPORT

Loud barks and bellows thunder through the sleeping block: '*Los! Los!* Fast! Fast!' The selection commission of three SS officers, two dogs, one
Lagerälteste, one *Blockälteste*, and an interpreter position themselves at the open wing of the gate.

'Get undressed and line up, single file, on the
right side of the partition! *Los!*'

All one thousand inmates of the block quickly
climb from four tiers of beds, pull off their dresses,
and line up alongside the brick structure that divides
the block in half, lengthwise.

'*Los!* Start moving ahead!'

It is very cold in the block. It has been raining all
night. Puddles cover the ground. The line of shivering, naked bodies advances towards the selection
commission and parades before them one by one.
Those who pass selection go through the open gate to
the outside and are ordered to dress. Those who do
not are ordered to drop their dresses in a pile at the
gate and return to the interior of the block, on the
other side of the partition. There they remain naked,
awaiting their fate.

By the time Mummy and I reach the gate, there is

a heap of sopping wet dresses on the ground, and a group of shivering bodies huddled together on the other side of the brick divider. I support Mummy with one hand as we advance, and, by the grace of God, she is able to manipulate the task without tottering. As we approach the commission, I make believe I am huddled against Mummy for warmth and not lending her my hand for support. The first SS man grabs her left arm and jerks her out of my grip. He looks over her body and shoves her roughly, impatiently out of the gate into the dark, foggy dawn slashed by relentless rain.

God, I must rush after her, keep her from falling. I restrain myself and keep my despair under masterly control while I stand stoically during the brief scrutiny. I'm stronger than Mummy. There's no doubt about me passing muster. Hurry. Hurry.

I am about to bolt through the gate, to reach Mummy, when one of the SS men notices the wound on my lower leg. It is the bruise I had received from a kick over three months ago, and it has been festering ever since. Now it is a deep hole oozing an awful dark brown liquid, and exuding an atrocious stench. Around the hole, the leg is swollen and red. Lately it has been quite painful.

The SS man pokes his colleague: 'Look at this.' He points to the wound on my leg. 'What do you think it is?'

Please, hurry. I must reach Mummy . . .

'I don't know. But it looks bad. She can't work with this. A week, and she'll be dead. *Tot!*'

'Drop your dress in the pile here, and join the others on the other side!'

'But, officer, please. That was my mother just before me. Let me go after her, please. Please. I'm strong. I can work hard. I promise, I will work very hard! Please let me go after my mother!'

'Shut up, *Schweinehund!* Get to the other side!'

I must go after Mummy. I must reach her right away.

I turn to the other SS man. He is young. Perhaps he will listen. 'Officer. Please. I *can* work. I'm very strong. This wound is nothing. Nothing. I've had it for over three months, and was doing heavy work in the mountains. *Planierung.* I am a good worker. I promise I will work even harder. Please . . . please, let me go after my mother.'

The young officer looks at me with disgust. With a snarl he points his stick and jabs me in the chest with such force that I stagger backwards. Then, without a word, he turns his back and continues the job of selection. And I am to join the naked group huddled at the back of the block.

I start to tremble violently. This cannot be happening. Mummy passed selection and I'm held back. In one cruel ironic quirk we both perish.

The others begin to comfort me. It's not so bad. Perhaps we will not be sent to the gas. Perhaps we will be sent to lighter labour. There will be other transports . . .

I'm not listening. I have to get to Mummy. I have to get to her before it's too late. She's out there in the pouring rain. She cannot stand on her feet without support. She cannot put on her dress without help. She's out there, lying in a puddle in the rain, naked. By now they must've discovered she was an invalid. By now they must've put her in a transport for the gas . . .

My head is spinning. My trembling grows more violent.

Now I recognize a girl I had worked with in Plaszow. She is the youngest of three sisters. The two older ones were sent on the transport, and now she is standing alone, visibly shivering and crying. I move over to her quickly, and whisper in her ear,

'Annie, let's sneak out of here and join the transport. Your sisters are there. Let's get to the transport . . .'

She is sobbing now, and does not answer. 'Come, Annie. Follow me. We can sneak through the back gate. No one will notice.'

'I'm afraid. They'll shoot us.'

I look around. No one is paying any attention to us. I run to the back gate. It's locked! The only means of escape is through the front gate.

At the front gate the selection is drawing to an end. The line on the other side of the partition is dwindling rapidly. The last inmates in line are disappearing through the open wing of the gate.

The *Blockälteste* approaches with a bundle of dresses in her hand. 'Here. You can put these on. Dress quickly. You'll be taken from here.'

It's all over. Under the *Blockälteste*'s watchful eye I pull a wet, soggy prison dress over my shivering body. She turns for a second. Like lightning I climb over the chest-high, brick partition, and duck for a moment. In a flash I yank off the dress, and dash to the end of the dwindling line.

There are three or four girls ahead of me. I clutch the dress to my right leg, concealing the wound. The sopping wet garment clings to my limb, entirely covering my lower leg. The SS men are in a hurry now. The selection has taken too long.

I'm last in line. I hold my breath.

A quick, cursive glance at my body, and the officer shoves me through the open gate into the downpour.

I look around. There is no one out here. The rain, like a sheet of lead, obliterates my vision. Where did everybody go? Where's Mummy?

The *Blockälteste* is closing the gate of our block. The selection commission, the SS men and their dogs, the *Lagerälteste* and their interpreter, are marching towards the SS command block.

I pull the prison uniform over my head. The selected transport is nowhere in sight. I run to the nearest block. It's dark and quiet. So is the one next to it. But the third block is lit and noisy. I run in there.

There is pandemonium in here. A stout woman stands on top of a table in the middle of the block, calling out numbers from a long sheet in her hand. Those whose numbers are called precipitate from the surging mass of women and form a line in the back of this block, which is much more enormous than ours.

I peruse the multitude, searching for a familiar face. Not one. I am afraid to ask questions. I'm afraid to inquire whether this is the transport freshly selected from Block 40.

Where can Mummy be? As the numbers line up in the back, the crowd lessens. I still cannot see Mummy. And I still do not see a familiar face.

The lines stand noisily for hours waiting for *Zählappell*. Finally the SS men arrive and begin the count.

It's late in the evening by the time we are given orders to march. The rain has subsided somewhat but has turned very cold. We march through the gate of the camp, past the command block where I knelt only a few days ago for twenty-four hours. We are marching on the road where the transport from Lodz arrived. I look for the yellow clown. It is not there.

We stand in formation outside the showers for over an hour. Where are we being taken? I have still not asked any questions. What is this transport that I have sneaked into? Where is it heading?

Perhaps Mummy's transport was lining up in another block while I rushed head-on into this one? Perhaps at this very moment Mummy's transport is being loaded on to trains, and shipped off who knows where? Or, perhaps she is, at this very moment, inside the showers, while we are awaiting our turn . . . What if she leaves through the other exit at the precise moment I am entering from this end? Or perhaps she was detected, and taken to the gas hours ago?

A ferocious trembling grips my body. What should I do now? I do not want to leave Auschwitz now. Perhaps Mummy was detected and held back in Auschwitz . . . not taken to the gas chambers yet. Perhaps I can still save her.

The front gates of the shower block open, we are hustled inside, and the doors shut behind us. There is no escape. There is no way out.

'Auskleiden! Los!' Get undressed. Move it!

In the crowded compartment, as bodies are getting stripped in haste, I notice a lone figure huddled motionlessly against the wall.

'Mummy!'

In a leap I am at her side. 'Mummy, it's you! It really is you! I can't believe it!'

Mummy is oblivious to my presence. She stares vacantly, her quaking body clinging to the wall. She seems desperately ill.

How did she get here? Who helped her dress, walk, line up? She cannot answer my questions.

Oh, God, I have found her. After all the panic, the tension, the fear . . . I have found her. She is here. Right here, in the showers. We are in the same transport. What perfect bliss!

We are together, Mummy and I. We are leaving Auschwitz together! What a divine miracle.

A Handkerchief

It is in shoes you conceal your possessions.

You have to leave your prison dress in a pile before entering the shower, and pick up a disinfected one from another pile at the exit. But you hold on to the shoes. You take them with you into the shower. It is in the shoes you hide things you hope to keep, like a small memento from home.

Mummy has such a memento. It's a small handkerchief with her initials embroidered in one corner. It was part of her trousseau. She wears it in her shoe, wrapped around her foot.

I help Mummy get undressed, and tuck the handkerchief in her shoe. We are driven into the shower compartment in a frantic haste. The rush of cold water from holes in the ceiling lasts less than five minutes.

'Los! Los! Blöde Hunde.' Move it! Idiotic bitches. Put on your shoes. Fast.

I struggle with my sopping wet shoes. By the time I am ready to help Mummy with hers, the room is almost empty. The tall, husky SS woman supervisor is standing in the doorway, driving the last few girls into the next compartment. Mummy is sitting on the wet floor clumsily trying to wrap the handkerchief about her foot. The SS woman notices her.

'*Du, blöde Hündin!* Hurry and get to the other room!'

But Mummy does not hear. She is oblivious to everything except the impossible task of manoeuvring the handkerchief around her foot with paralysed hands. The SS woman leaps at her, grabs her arm, and in a rage begins to twist it.

I lose my head. I forget everything. I remember only that Mummy's arm is paralysed, that she is ill and very weak, and that the SS woman is going to break her arm.

I jump at the tall, husky woman and shove her against the wall. 'Leave my mother alone! Don't you see you are going to break her arm?'

The towering buxom figure in the dreaded SS uniform swings around. Her fist on my cheek sends me reeling. A second punch knocks me to the slippery floor. Now she is on top of me. She is kicking me in the face, in the chest, in the abdomen. She is kicking my head. The black boots gleam and my blood splashes thinly on the wet floor. A kick in the back sends me rolling across the floor towards the exit. Then the door slams and I'm lying flat on the cold, slick floor. Cold drops of water keep falling on my face from somewhere.

A thought formulates somehow – I'm alive! I taste blood. I am unable to lift my head. My body feels totally numb. But I am alive. She did not trample me to death. She could have shot me. But she did not. I have committed the unthinkable, the unforgivable. I attacked an SS officer. The gravest possible form of sabotage . . . Yet I am alive. Brutally bruised, but alive.

The noise in the adjacent compartment has subsided. I hear Mummy's faint voice, 'Elli . . . Ellikém. Can you hear me? Try to get up. Try. Can you hear me? Elli, try. I cannot help you.

You must. You must get up. Now. All by yourself.'

I roll on my abdomen and slowly pull myself up. My head reels. Blood is trickling from my nose and mouth. I cannot open my left eye. There is a very sharp pain in my left side. But my legs are not broken. I can stand.

Slowly I limp out of the damp compartment. In a puddle in the middle of the room I notice a dismal-looking little cloth. It's Mummy's handkerchief.

'Mummy, wait.' I stagger towards the puddle and pick up the small, soggy rag.

'Leave it there.' Mummy's voice is an agonized whimper of resignation. 'I don't want it any more.'

'But *I* want it.'

In the next room I manage to put on a dress, and help Mummy put on hers, and join the lines of women shivering in the cold dark September night.

We stand outside the showers till dawn. All night we stand with freshly shaven heads, wet bodies, in threadbare grey cotton uniforms. There is no means of protection from the relentless autumn wind. The brick wall of the block has no nooks or crevices to cling to. The cold is inexorable. It seems unbearable, this exposure to cold, hunger, fatigue.

Many girls begin to sob aloud. Others whimper with teeth clenched. And some recite phrases remembered from the Psalms.

The pain in my side grows sharper. My left cheek is swollen. The cut above my lip makes it difficult to speak. The old wound in my right leg is throbbing with a vengeance. I'm unable to stand on that leg.

There is an especially painful bump on the back of my head. Mummy says I fell to the stone floor of the shower room with a frightful bang. And then the SS woman gave a sharp kick to that same spot on my head. But my head did not crack. Solid material, Daddy used to tease. Solid, like rock. And stubborn like rock.

'You are insane,' several girls accost me on the lines. 'Totally insane. Didn't you know what you were doing? You jumped on an SS woman! And she didn't kill you!'

I crouch against the wall of the block near Mummy, who is slumped, unconscious, on the ground. I drape an arm about her skeletal shoulders and huddle close to keep us warm. Her open mouth is a dark hollow.

The SS guards have retired for the night to a nearby block, and we are left on our own. Everyone takes the liberty of crouching. The night seems forbidding and endless. The sky has not a single star.

The filtering light of dawn brings our German masters marching briskly. The roll call brings the reality of our existence into focus. We have survived the night.

A long row of cattle trucks await us at the train station. I help Mummy, slowly, painfully, up into the wagon. Then I climb up, smothering a cry of pain. A sense of triumph overwhelms the anguish. I have won. I have attained the first, and greatest, triumph of my life.

My whole being is awash with a sense of gratitude.

THIS MUST BE HEAVEN

AUGSBURG, 3 SEPTEMBER 1944

'Elli, wake up. We've arrived.'

Sun streaks into the truck through open doors. The train stands still. Mummy is gently shaking my shoulder.

I can open only one eye. My head weighs a ton. Slowly I scramble to a sitting position.

'You slept for over twenty-four hours,' Mummy says. 'We've arrived.'

'Where are we?'

'The sign says Augsburg.'

Augsburg. Augsburg. I learned about Augsburg in school. The battle of Augsburg. When was it? When was the battle of Augsburg?

German officers, men and women, stand on the platform and scrutinize us with curious glances. They stare at us, then exchange incredulous, puzzled looks.

The tall officer at the head of the group breaks the awkward silence, and addresses us directly: 'We expected women. Five hundred women.' Then, after several moments' hesitation, he inquires, 'Who is in charge?'

Our guards had returned with the departing

train. We have no escort, no leaders. Except these openly astonished, hesitant men and women in an unfamiliar military uniform. They are our new masters.

'Any of you speak German?' the officer inquires again.

Several girls volunteer.

'We expected a transport of women from Auschwitz,' the tall officer repeats. 'Are you from Auschwitz? Were you sent instead of the women?'

'We are from Auschwitz. And we are women.'

A wave of disbelief ripples through the ranks of the assembled army personnel. Women? Our freshly shaven heads, grey prison garb, and sticklike bodies are not very convincing proof.

We quickly line up in rows of five, ready to march. Our new masters just stand, waiting. We too stand, awaiting the order to march.

The train pulls out of the station, and the last wagon has disappeared around the bend, and we are still standing at attention. Finally, the commandant addresses us again, *'Aber wo sind eure Pakete?'* But where is your luggage? Laughter rings from the lines. Our luggage?

'We have no luggage, *Herr Offizier*,' the interpreter says softly. 'We have nothing.'

'Tell him, our valets are bringing our luggage on another train.' The wisecrack in Hungarian is greeted by a general cackle. Hungarian is the language of all five hundred of us.

Wisecracks begin to fly.

'My luggage is being sent special delivery.'

'Oh, I forgot my golf clubs in Auschwitz!'

Laughter is breaking up the lines.

'You have no luggage at all? No personal belongings? How can that be?' The officer is incredulous.

'No,' the interpreter says, then, her tone lowered, she repeats, 'We have nothing.'

We march through clean provincial streets. Houses, neat little gardens, cobblestoned streets. People are gawking at us from windows. The few passers-by on the street turn to look at us in astonishment.

Houses. People. Trams. My God, life still goes on. Despite Auschwitz. Despite gas chambers.

Mummy drags her feet. She is unable to keep up with the pace of the march. A short, blonde woman officer approaches her. 'What is your name?' she asks timidly.

'My name?' Mummy begins to stammer. 'A-17361.'

'But that's a number. What is your name?'

'You want my *name?*'

'Yes. What's your name?'

'Laura Friedmann.'

'Frau Friedmann, can you walk a little faster?' Mrs Friedmann? She actually called Mummy by her name, and with a title – Frau? Mrs? Am I dreaming?

'No. I am unable to walk faster. Even this is great effort. I received an injury in Auschwitz. I'm partially paralysed.'

I hope it's safe to say all this to a German officer, even though she is obviously not SS. Neither are the others. They wear the uniform of the *Wehrmacht*, the official German army.

'Do not worry,' the German officer replies. 'Here you will get better. We will take good care of you.'

I am surely dreaming.

At the terminal we are loaded on to trams reserved for us then driven through busy city traffic to the industrial section. Here we disembark at the gate of a factory complex with large black lettering: MICHELWERKE.

Michelwerke is a factory complex manufacturing parts for the *Luftwaffe*, the German air force. In order to boost production, the plant had requested five hundred female prison workers from a concentration camp. And here we are.

Our living quarters are in one of the factory buildings. First we are led to the showers in the basement. There are real metal showerheads here, not just holes in the ceiling. There are wooden mats on the floor, and taps marked 'warm' and 'cold'. We are handed a clean towel each! And soap. One piece of soap to every one of us! Towels and soap!

'Girls, my soap is perfumed!'

'Mine, too!'

'Girls, this is a dream.'

'We've landed in paradise.'

'This cannot be true. We are making it all up . . .'

You yourself turn on the water. Warm water comes from the tap marked 'warm'. And you turn it off when you've finished. At your leisure. It does not start and stop by an unseen arbitrary hand. In this shower you are your own master. And the towel. It's clean and soft.

As we get out of the showers, a secret spark of self-esteem is nurtured deep within. It's a divine message. A promise of redemption. A message of faith. Of hope.

We sit around long tables in the yard and are served warm soup. The soup is golden yellow with long yellow noodles in white, clean porcelain bowls. Real food in real dishes.

Several girls begin to weep. They weep silently, and their tears trickle into the bowls of steaming soup. They weep and the warm liquid soothes their parched eager lips. Their aching souls.

After soup, there is more. A second course. It's dumplings

with sauerkraut. Their flavour surpasses anything I've ever eaten.

But it does not satiate my appetite. My craving for more and more food is intensified. When the meal is over, my stomach still smarts with hunger. But my soul soars to heaven.

Mummy shares my yearning for a quantity of food. But she also shares my joy in the quality of the food.

After dinner, our new masters escort us to our living quarters on the sixth floor. We receive three large rooms, airy and light, with individual, double-tiered bunk beds. On each bed there is a straw sack covered with a sheet. A clean, white sheet!

This must be heaven.

What will tomorrow bring?

Herr Zerkübel

AUGSBURG, SEPTEMBER 1944

Here we are, a singular workforce – five hundred young women, most in their twenties, new arrivals from Auschwitz. We are concentration-camp inmates – starved, bruised, brutalized.

The reception in Augsburg left us breathless with its hints of humanity, with its promise of hope.

We are lined up in the factory yard, to be sorted out for our work assignments. A white-coated, heavy-set man with short-cropped, flaming red hair approaches us. His eyes are blue as ice and just as cold; his face is a frozen mask of unsmiling gravity. He is Herr Zerkübel, the director of the factory division, the lord and master of our new world. In a tone barely audible yet unerring in its force, he commands us to step out of line, one by one, and proceeds to inspect us. He subjects each one individually to a most curious scrutiny, peering deep into eyes, measuring the distance between eyes, eyebrows and cheekbones, and the height and width of foreheads with a small pocket ruler. I can barely control my shivering.

Tall, blonde, fair-skinned girls with blue or green eyes are commanded to step aside. There are eight of us.

Now Herr Zerkübel adds somewhat shorter girls

with blonde hair, blue or green eyes, and fair skin. He needs thirty-five in this group, he says. Finally, he adds redheads, and even girls with light brown hair. But all have light eyes and fair skin.

This is a select group for *Montage*. Work in *Montage* requires superior intelligence, he explains. Herr Zerkübel determines superior intellect by the colours of hair, skin and eyes. The colours of the Aryan race.

The next category consists of girls with brown hair and eyes, but fair skin. They are assigned less complex, more routine metalwork, in the *Dreherei*. The black-haired, dark-eyed women, among them a noted physicist, a doctor and a college professor, are assigned the most primitive task of polishing metal parts in the *Lackiererei*.

Herr Zerkübel departs with a barely perceptible nod in the direction of our military masters, and they escort us to our living quarters. Now the rooms are reassigned, according to rank. The *Montage* girls receive the brightest of the three rooms. With beds quite far apart, our room has an air of spaciousness, while the other two are somewhat crowded, and somewhat darker. Although she is assigned to the *Putzkommando*, Mummy is allowed to join me in the *Montage* quarters. We occupy two adjacent bunks on the lowest tier.

The next day we are roused at dawn for *Zählappell* and breakfast – black coffee and a piece of brown bread. The line-up for work takes place in three groups, *Montage*, *Dreherei* and *Lackiererei*.

Just as the lady officer had promised, in Augsburg Mummy is recuperating. Her task of cleaning floors and windows is designed to help her recover. As no one supervises her, she gets a chance to rest. Rest is her only cure. Although she receives no other medical treatment, her condition begins to improve.

Gradually she starts to regain the use of her right hand. Her left hand, however, remains partially paralysed. Her walk also begins to improve. Little by little she recovers her sense of balance and begins to walk unaided. Slowly, very slowly, she starts to carry out her tasks in the *Putzkommando*, to clean windows and wash floors.

Her posture remains permanently altered. Her head is bent forward almost as sharply as when the accident occurred. And her walk is slow, deliberate and uneven. But we are free of the imminent threat of the gas chamber.

Herr Zerkübel is the supreme lord of *Montage*. At ten o'clock every morning, like clockwork, he emerges from his glass enclosure in the centre of *Montage*. Like Zeus's descent from Mount Olympus, Herr Zerkübel's approach with measured steps and erect posture, his silent scrutiny of our every move, inspires awe. Not a muscle moves in his face, not a flicker of an eye betrays any human sentiment. Never does he give any indication that he even notices our presence.

When he was displeased, Herr Zerkübel would ensconce himself in the glass office, summon our guard and have him escort the culprit into his exalted and terrible presence for a reprimand. The reprimand was always delivered to a point above the unfortunate creature's head, in scathing negation of her existence.

Work in the *Montage* is interesting. Here we produce a compact, intricate gadget, the ultimate result of having assembled many little parts. These small parts are cut out in the *Dreherei*, finished, polished and painted in the *Lackiererei*, and then brought to us in the *Montage* to be assembled into a precision instrument that is supposed to control the distance and direction of the bomb ejected by a fighter plane.

I work on three small machines, combining minute parts

into a fascinating unit. The completed instrument is like a medium-sized camera studded with colourful wires and screws in an intricate pattern.

We work in an assembly line, all thirty-five of us, each affixing one or two small components to the growing gadget.

Only four or five German civilians work in the *Montage*. Their job is to test the more complex sections before the gadget progresses too far. Mr Scheidel's machine, for instance, checks the accuracy of my work. He inserts the unit I produce into his machine, and it indicates if I have made a mistake. If I have, the entire unit has to be discarded – an inexcusable waste. Mistakes are chalked up as deliberate acts of negligence. Or worse: sabotage.

The completed gadget reaches the glass office. But first it is checked and rechecked by two German civilian experts. Herr Zerkübel is not to be troubled by mistakes. But we are aware that he sees everything from his glass dominion; he knows of every mishap, no matter how minor. We are aware, and we live in a constant state of dread.

The final product reaches Herr Zerkübel's glass office with an assumption of perfection. He receives each instrument with ceremonial formality, and inserts it into his sophisticated checking apparatus. All the minute parts of the gadget are then set in motion and begin to move in harmonious complexity, sending a fine set of whirring and ticking sounds like discreet bells through the entire expanse of the *Montage*. It is a proud sound, a happy sound. The instrument is working perfectly, and we made it. We have created something intricate, and complex, and difficult.

It is also a tragic sound. The success of our work contributes to the success of the German war effort. We are toiling against ourselves.

Leah Kohn, Forgive Me . . .

AUGSBURG, WINTER 1944/1945

I shudder at the sight of the familiar SS uniform.

After the arrival of the new SS officer from Dachau, a concentration camp nearby, our little haven of hope is gone. A radical transformation has taken place in Augsburg. Five days of fragile bliss are over.

The white sheets have been removed from our bunk beds and now we sleep on bare straw sacks. The food has turned into a nondescript, tasteless mush. The table and the benches have been taken away, and now we eat our food crouching on beds or sitting on the floor in the corridor. And there is *Zählappell* twice a day.

The most painful transformation is in the attitude of our German staff. Their friendliness has turned to curtness and, in some, to animosity. Two days after the arrival of the SS man, one of our guards called us *blöde Hunde*, idiotic bitches, and we quivered with the familiarity of the epithet. Instead of looking at us, our guards started to avert their eyes. They started to shout orders. And some started to carry whips.

The commandant of the camp, the *Oberscharführer*, has remained fair. One evening while shovelling snow in the yard, we discover mounds in which potatoes are stored for the winter. We quickly dig them up and, hiding them under our dresses, smuggle enough potatoes into the camp to allow each inmate at least one potato. We wash them in the toilet and eagerly await our bedtime. Only after lights-out do we dare consume our concealed delicacies. Noiselessly, with utmost care, so as not to attract the attention of the guard on patrol we bite into the hard, delightful skin of the raw potato. But Mummy saves her potato. 'For Sabbath lights,' she says. Friday at sunset Mummy kindles her Sabbath lights in the carved-out potato halves using oil smuggled from the factory and threads from our blanket for wicks. But moments after she whispers the Sabbath benediction over the faintly flickering lights, the *Oberscharführer* enters. The room is dark; only the light from the potato on the windowsill illuminates the tall bunk beds and the frightened faces of the young girls who have gathered to hear Mummy's blessing for the holy day.

'What's this?' His tone is exceptionally gruff. He approaches the window and turns to face the cluster of young women frozen in fright. 'Whose is this?' No one speaks. Mummy calls out in a low voice. 'They're mine, *Herr Oberscharführer*. I lit those lights. For Sabbath.' The *Oberscharführer*'s eyes, as they scan our faces, are torches of rage. His voice cuts like steel. 'Lights in the window! Do you know what you've committed? You!' he shouts at Mummy. 'Take these away at once!'

Mummy slowly picks up the burning potato halves and follows the *Oberscharführer* out the door. At the exit, the *Oberscharführer* turns and issues a stern warning: 'This should never happen again!' He orders Mummy to put out the lights in the toilet and dump the potatoes into the dustbin. Thank

God. He does not ask where the oil and potatoes came from. And he does not punish us. We are lucky.

The holiday of Hanukkah is in ten days'. The incident inspires us to save potatoes for a Hanukkah celebration with lights. But we have learned our lesson. Before lighting the Hanukkah oil lamps in carved-out potato halves, we post look-outs at each entrance and develop a system of warning signals. A miracle comes to pass. For eight days we delight in kindling lights and singing Hanukkah songs without being caught.

Soon after our arrival the *Oberscharführer* said our uniforms were unsuitable for winter and put in an order for clothes for us. We had arrived in the regulation grey prison dresses with two large red letters, K and L, painted on our backs. The letters stand for the words *Konzentrations Lager* – Concentration Camp.

The dresses, coats and sweaters have arrived. They are lovely, colourful clothes – not sacklike prison uniforms meant for camp inmates, but garments to be worn by young women.

Our happiness knows no bounds. The new clothes have transformed us from nonentities into people. From sexless, ageless, shapeless digits into – girls! The clothes have given us dimensions.

Some of the girls brush their budding hair with wet fingers into provocative styles, pinch their cheeks to achieve surprisingly becoming complexions, and assume graceful postures. The effect is quite startling.

I have received a pink dress made of soft wool and an elegant warm tweed coat with a sumptuous deep brown fur collar. As I wrap it about me, I feel luxuriously pampered. It has a rich texture and a beautiful cut, and it makes me look like a young woman. It hugs and comforts my thin, long, bony body, and makes it feel and look better nourished. In the coat I look lanky rather than gaunt.

The excitement keeps me from falling asleep. As the coat lies at the foot of my bed, I keep reaching over and stroking the soft fabric with my fingers and brushing the soft fur against my cheeks.

In the morning I stand for *Zählappell* in my new pink dress, then go off to work in the *Montage* wearing it. Mr Scheidel, the old German civilian who works next to me, stops in his tracks as he approaches. He does not recognize me at first. The smile of recognition in his face, the surprised look in his eyes, reveals the extent of change in my appearance. And I feel like a human being.

I feel like a person in my pink dress. My outlook on life has changed. Old Mr Scheidel's reaction, the reaction of a free individual, a German civilian from the real world, is of paramount importance. His look of approval validates my new self-image. It re-creates my world.

All the other girls also sit self-consciously at their workbenches and giggle in secret anticipation of Herr Zerkübel's reaction. At ten, Herr Zerkübel, the supreme master of *Montage*, makes his customary, silent, impassive appearance. As he passes among the rows of young girls fidgeting in suppressed excitement, his demeanour remains aloof. His stony face and posture continue to hold immutable disregard of our very being. Our new clothes do not render us visible to Herr Zerkübel.

Herr Zerkübel's manner does not dampen my enthusiasm. I sense a change in my old partner, Mr Scheidel, and that's enough.

In the evening, back at our living quarters, I try on my coat again. It's beautiful!

All at once, I notice white stitching at the hem of the lining. I look closer, and see that the stitches form letters. LEAH KOHN – DÉS. It's a name and a place. A town in Hungary. And the name of a girl. A Jewish girl.

These clothes belonged to Jewish women. They were taken away from them, and given to us! This coat . . . this coat belonged to Leah Kohn from Dés. She was tall and slim, just like me. And she loved this coat, that's why she stitched her name into the hem of the lining.

Is she alive? Is she now shivering on bitter cold winter days and nights in a thin prison sack, while I delight in her warm coat?

Or was she taken to the gas chamber to suffocate in agony after having been stripped of this beautiful coat?

Leah Kohn's coat is no longer a source of delight for me. It has become an agonizing burden. And so has the pretty pink dress of a nameless owner.

I have become an accomplice to SS brutality and plunder by wearing these clothes. I have become a participant in Nazi crimes by benefiting from pillage and perhaps even murder. How dare I wear this coat? How dare I wear this dress?

Leah Kohn, forgive me.

The Bowl of Soup

The 'Goat' is especially nervous this morning. This SS man looks like a goat and even his gait is like that of the foolish animal. His large, buck teeth protrude above a pointed chin and, when he walks, his head bobs up and down on a ludicrously elongated neck, like a goat. And the name has stuck.

At the *Zählappell* he announces that he needs forty girls to clear some debris in the factory yard. Some debris! We knew there was extensive damage in the wake of yesterday's Allied bombing. Our factory was put out of operation for today. We could see from our cell-block windows that the passage to the factory was blocked by masonry fragments, twisted metal parts, and other rubble – the remains of the factory annex levelled last night.

The frequency and intensity of the bombings heighten our anticipation. We feel that the Allies have the upper hand. The end of the war just has to be near. The taste of liberation is becoming ever more tangible. And with growing hope, fear of death becomes an actuality. There is palpable tension in the air.

From one end of the roll call, the Goat separates

eight rows and orders them to march. I am among them. It is a brutally cold morning. Fierce wind slaps frozen snow piles against the windowpanes. The ground, where exposed by snowdrifts, glistens with patches of ice.

At a run we head for our cell block to get the coats we had been issued at the beginning of the winter. But the Goat is frantic. He orders us to march straight outdoors.

'*Los!*' he shouts, in a nervous rage. 'Follow me. March!'

This is insane. We have nothing on but a thin dress and a pair of shoes. No underwear or stockings. It is certain death to work outdoors without at least our threadbare coats.

As a rule the Goat is not extraordinarily cruel to us. As a matter of fact, I have reason to believe I owe him my life. The incident happened last Yom Kippur, when I decided to observe this holy day of fast. I had to forgo my food ration before leaving for work on the night shift because it was served after the onset of the fast. Naturally, I also refused the midnight soup and the morning bread portion. The next evening meal was served before the conclusion of Yom Kippur, so I left for the second night of work after having fasted for thirty-six hours. At 11. p.m., one hour before the anticipated midnight bowl of soup, I collapsed, unconscious, next to my machine. When I came too I was peering into the worried blue eyes of the Goat. I was told it was he who had carried me to the factory medical office and then, without reporting the incident, escorted me back to work.

But this morning his demeanour was changed. The cauldron of breakfast coffee arrived, but he did not allow us even to have the hot drink.

'But our coats, *bitte*, Herr Offizier, let us quickly get our coats. It'll take only a minute. *Bitte?*'

'*Los!*' he shouts, beside himself. 'March after me this instant!'

He heads for the staircase. We march at his heels. As we pass the toilet, several girls duck through its doors. I follow them. We hide behind the tall wastebins in the toilet.

When he reaches the ground level, the Goat counts his group and discovers that eight of us are missing. In his panic he orders the column back to the camp. The *Oberscharführer* is notified, and a campwide search is mounted for the missing girls.

All this time we are crouching behind the wastebins. From the sounds reaching the toilet we realize what is going on, and hold our breath. Soon one of our inmates enters the toilet and calls out, 'Come out, girls. The *Oberscharführer* is very angry. He ordered the entire camp to go without rations if you don't come out immediately.'

We file out of the toilet. The *Oberscharführer* barks the order: 'Line up against the wall. Attention! Not a move, till midnight.'

All day, all evening, in the hall, without food, without moving. It is bad news, but not as bad as it might have been.

We do not have to do the work outdoors. And the others are issued sweaters in addition to coats.

As we stand there I am terribly hungry. It is the fifth day of Passover. Mummy and I had decided that one of us would observe Passover by not eating the bread ration. The other one would compensate for the bread by sharing her ration of the cooked meal at noon and in the evening. I had volunteered to be the one to give up the bread ration. Mummy had agreed because she was in far worse physical shape than I.

So I had only black coffee in the morning, and one and a half bowls of soup at noon and in the evening. All that liquid without the ration of solid bread made me ravenously hungry, and by the third day of Passover I felt quite weak. Now, on the fifth day, having been deprived even of the morning coffee, I am feeling faint. My leg wound, which has become much smaller, now starts to hurt. I find it difficult to stand but am afraid to crouch, even when the Germans are not looking. I dare not attempt a second violation.

Some of us begin tottering but dare not collapse. Our camp mates are neither permitted to speak to us nor to make gestures of communication. They pass by and cast compassionate glances at us. Poor Mummy keeps walking back and forth, passing me every few minutes, her face a mask of pity and despair. I make an effort to encourage her, but as the hours pass this proves almost impossible. I think I will pass out at any minute.

At noon the cauldron of soup is distributed in the hall right before our noses. So is the evening soup and bread. We are still standing. My legs feel wooden and my spine is a stripe of pain. My stomach feels like a ton of bricks. There is a light trembling in my whole body. I am very cold.

At 10 p.m. the camp retires for the night. Lights go out on the entire floor. Only a faint searchlight illuminates the corridor. Our shoulders slump. Our heads hang to one side. Our lips and our hands tremble. We are beyond fatigue. Beyond hunger. But we are still standing.

Brisk footsteps approach. It is the *Oberscharführer*.

'Are you tired? Are you hungry? Did you learn your lesson?'

We begin to cry.

'Go to your blocks!'

We are barely able to move. Slowly, we trudge to our respective cells.

It is dark and quiet in my cell block. Noiselessly, I approach my bed. Mummy stirs. She sits up abruptly and hugs me with uncharacteristic vehemence. 'Thank God! Thank God it's over! Come, sit here.'

From under her blanket she takes out a bowl. There is soup in it. The bowl is almost to the brim with thick, cold soup. It was her supper. And her lunch. She had saved it for me.

'Eat it.'

'It is your lunch and supper. I will eat half. Take out your spoon, and let's eat together.'

'No. I will not eat. You have not eaten all day. You have to eat it all.'

'Look, Mummy. I admit, I'm very hungry. And I will eat half of the soup. But you must eat the other half because you have become very thin and every drop of food you deny yourself may prove disastrous. Take your spoon and let's eat together.'

She gets very angry. She whispers, 'Stop talking and eat!'

She takes the spoon, thrusts it into the soup and raises it to my mouth. I shake my head with lips shut tight. Mummy looks straight into my eyes, her face aflame. But I am adamant: 'I will not eat if you don't share it with me.'

Mummy's anger and despair charges the air. 'If you won't eat it, I'll empty the bowl on top of the bed!'

I shake my head. 'I will eat only if you also eat.'

Mummy takes the bowl of soup and turns it over. In a splash, the contents land on top of her grey army blanket. Pieces of potato scatter in every direction. The liquid is sucked up by the bedding.

I cannot believe my eyes.

The soup. There is no soup! Mummy deliberately spilled it. And on the bed! My God, what is happening to us?

'Mummy, why did you do this? For God's sake, Mummy, why?'

Mummy begins to cry. She hugs me tight, and cries. We lie down on my side of the narrow cot. I also begin to cry. For the soup, for Mummy, for all the hungry, miserable, cold prisoners of the world.

We cry until dawn. Our weeping is uncomforting, heavy and hopeless. Bitterness burns my throat. Unrelieved, oppressive, desperate. The sky seems to darken with the coming of the dawn. Our grief is total, and for the first time, uncontrollable.

Much later we find out that was the night Daddy died – on the fifth day of Passover.

THE BIRD OF GOLD

AUGSBURG, 2 APRIL 1945

For some unfathomable reason, on this dark dawn in the spring of 1945, I remember a strange dream I had over a year ago.

My father and I, the two of us, stood in the middle of our storage room called the *kamra*. In this room we kept sacks of flour, animal feed, chopped-up wood, and other odds and ends.

I hated the *kamra*. It was a dark, bleak place. When Mother sent me to fetch flour or wood, I hurried out of the *kamra* as fast as I could. When I was little, I used to believe there were evil spirits in the dark corners of the *kamra* and was terrified to enter it.

But in my dream I was standing in the middle of the *kamra* with my father, without an apparent purpose. We just stood there, silently, our backs to the entrance where a dim light filtered in. The flour sacks stood menacingly against the wall, and the pile of wood harboured a strange, brooding stillness.

Suddenly, a bird flew into the *kamra*. An unusual bird with an egg-shaped body covered with golden feathers and large, greenish yellow wings. As it flew in, a shaft of bright light streamed in with it. The shaft of light followed the bird as it fluttered about.

It hovered above my father's head, the light growing ever brighter until it bathed the bird in a glittering flood of blinding sparkle.

But the room remained cloaked in darkness. And we, too, my father and I, remained wrapped in the shadows.

'Look at that bird!' my father called out, pale with shock. He was deeply moved. Not frightened; strangely moved by the awesome sight. I glanced at the bird and then averted my eyes. I dared not look at it. It was too awesome, too frightening. I began to tremble. My father gripped my arm, and again cried, 'Look at that bird!'

He stood transfixed, not moving his gaze from the horrible beauty of the apparition. His grip tightened on my arm. When I looked at him, he was no longer a living creature but a grey statue with eyes lifted to the heights. His lips, motionless, kept whispering, 'Look at that bird . . .'

When I awoke I had a clear, dreadful knowledge that my father would be dead. I did not tell anyone of my dream. I did not ever think of that dream.

Until now. And now, all of a sudden, the dream takes hold of me with the savagery of the dark, bitter-cold dawn.

An Echo in the Fog

EN ROUTE TO DACHAU, 3–4 APRIL 1945

Fantastic rumours are circulating during the last days of March. The Allies are approaching. Our liberators, the Americans and the British, are very near . . .

Then other rumours reach us. We are going to be evacuated. Shipped eastward. We are going to be transported to Austria . . .

There is nothing to indicate the rumours' validity. Our work routine is the same. There is no change at the factory. None of the German workers reveal any awareness of imminent events. No covert remarks of regret come from Mr Scheidel, who has become my friend. Nothing.

Then, one April morning at the conclusion of *Zählappell*, the *Oberscharführer* reads the order. Tomorrow morning we are to be transported to Dachau under guard. Not a word of this is to be discussed with anyone. Not in camp. Not at work.

The day laden with apprehension drags on. Mr Scheidel is oblivious of my predicament. Why can't I say goodbye to him? Why can't I convey my fears . . . or my thanks for the surreptitious help?

I remember the morning when he put a small brown paper bag on the workbench and hinted with a wink that I take it. There were dried thin bread crusts in the bag. When I attempted to thank him, he averted his eyes in panic and acted feverishly preoccupied with work. I hid the brown bag under my dress on the way back to camp, and Mummy and I eagerly shared the marvellous snack. His gesture encouraged me to ask him for paper. 'Paper?' His astonishment had baffled and worried me. 'Did you say paper? What kind of paper? What do you need paper for?' I knew it was risky to ask for anything, especially an item like paper, but had not realized the extent of its gravity. I regretted my mistake but was obliged to answer his question.

'Any paper. Just a small piece. For writing.'

'For writing? What do you want to write?'

'A poem. I want to write a poem. I . . . some time ago I used to write poems. But forgive me. I didn't intend to . . .'

'Ah, a poem. You're a poet, ha? A poet!' Mr Scheidel's rasping laughter frightened me.

But the next morning he furtively placed a few yellow slips of paper wrapped in crumpled brown paper on my lap under the workbench. This was the onset of Mr Scheidel's clandestine paper-smuggling operation, and the onset of my career as camp poet.

Goodbye, Mr Scheidel, faded old friend. Goodbye, *Montage*. And you, Herr Zerkübel, the monument of stony superiority. As you emerge from your glass enclosure, will you notice that we are gone?

The journey through Augsburg is a high point. Our tram snakes around Gothic buildings lining the cobblestoned streets. The city is gradually receding into a fine spring mist, which seems to envelop every silhouette of the past.

Goodbye, Augsburg. I had hoped you would be the scene of

our liberation. I had dreamed countless times of Allied troops marching towards me on your cobblestoned streets, bringing liberty with the rattle of armoured trucks and tanks. I had a sweet, mysterious premonition of freedom when I first caught sight of your Gothic charm, when I first breathed your reassuring civilized air seven months ago. Seven months of dogged dreams, hopes and prayers.

Now we are leaving you, Mummy and I, and all of us, still prisoners. Heading for what future? Dachau. What awaits us in Dachau?

At the terminal we disembark, and continue on foot. Our journey leads through bombed-out streets, gutted neighbourhoods. The last seven months have not left the city unscathed.

The railway station is also in ruins. The row of cattle trucks is far beyond. We wade through heaps of rubble to reach them. The train takes off instantly. By nightfall we arrive at a gloomy, dark place called Landsberg, and we march along a narrow rocky road through stark landscape, past barren trees, endless telephone poles. In the gathering dusk flocks of crows perched on the telephone wires are strikingly etched against a metallic sky. Their shrill cries send a chill down my spine.

Camp Landsberg is a subsidiary of Dachau, a sprawling, enormous camp, but its austere gates do not open for us. The camp is full to capacity: inmates from several other camps in the vicinity arrived before us. We are lined up near the gate, and wait far into the night. Our guards telephone for orders, and during the early dawn the orders reach us. Back to the cattle trucks.

Thank God, we are leaving this ominous place.

During the late afternoon the train halts at a place called Mühldorf. Open trucks are awaiting us at the station, and we are driven among tended green fields and then through the gates of a small, overcrowded camp. Skeletal inmates flock noisily to meet us with huge, hysterical eyes, eager faces, and rapid, animated questions. What camp are we coming from? What have we been doing there? Where are we from, originally? They are women, emaciated beyond anything we have seen. Even the inmates at Landsberg, who had flocked to the fence and whose shrivelled appearances had shocked us, were not so starved as these excited skeletons. They speak with rasping voices, clamouring for answers and more answers.

Soon we find out that typhus raged at Mühldorf and at all the other camps of the Dachau complex all winter long. It was this devastating disease that killed about fifty people daily, and left the survivors in such a skeletal state.

The male inmates behind the barbed-wire fence look even more ravaged. In less than an hour we find out that there are men from Somorja, our hometown, among them. And a bit of heaven – Bubi, my brother, is in Waldlager, Mühldorf's twin camp in the nearby forest!

Mummy and I can barely contain our excitement. How can we get to meet Bubi? We find out that trucks with provisions go to Waldlager daily, and if we are lucky we might be picked for the unloading brigade. If we persist in volunteering for this physically taxing assignment, we might eventually be selected to go along with the trucks.

The next morning one hundred women are selected for transfer to Waldlager. Mummy and I are among them! Right after *Zählappell* we are put on trucks and driven through luscious green woods. The sun's rays and a dainty breeze dapple the greenery, and I feel happiness tremble within me. Mummy and I are in ecstasy. Everything is turning out beautifully. Oh, my dear God. Thank you, my dear God!

Waldlager looks like a forest of oversized mushrooms. Hundreds of small, grassy mounds conceal an underground world of bunkers, where thousands of inmates are housed, fifty to each long burrow.

Our dark, dank hole is lit by a small window in the ceiling, which, just like the entrance of the bunker, is camouflaged by tall grass. In our excitement, Mummy and I can think only of Bubi. We find out that the men's camp is right beyond the barbed-wire fence we saw nearby, and when the guards' backs are turned it is possible to meet the men and even talk to them after work and the evening *Zählappell*.

Mummy and I spend the day anxiously waiting for nightfall.

Finally, after *Zählappell*, we stand by the fence, huddled together against a relentless downpour. The entire camp is shrouded in haze and no living soul seems to stir on the other side of the fence. Just as Mummy and I resolve to make our way back to our bunker, two sticklike figures materialize from the mist and slowly approach the fence. One of them mutters in Yiddish, his voice barely projecting across the fence, 'Are you from the new transport?'

'Yes.'

'From which camp?'

'From an aeroplane factory in Augsburg.'

'You must have had it good there. You look strong. Where are you from?'

'Czechoslovakia. Hungarian territory. Somorja is the town's name.'

'There are some men here from Somorja.'

'We've heard. That's why we're here,' Mummy says, and her voice rises in anticipation. 'Do you know my son, Bubi

Friedmann? Tall. Blond. He was an interpreter in Auschwitz. Do you know him?'

'Yes, we know him. He's in a bunker together with others from Somorja. Wait here. We will tell him to come.'

The two figures disappear with a slow, shuffling gait into the milky darkness, and we are left standing in the brutally cold rain. The barbed-wire fence looms like an eerie black web, with hanging raindrops forever uniting and dripping into dark pools on the ground. The piece of bread from Lina is becoming soggy and wet in Mummy's hand.

Lina was assigned to the kitchen commando this morning, and she smuggled the bread from the kitchen. She gave it to Mummy during the *Zählappell*. 'Mrs Friedmann, give this to your son when you see him tonight. The men in this camp get very little food.'

Out of the gloom a tall, thin shape now emerges and comes toward us. Ah, Bubi! But when he is nearer we see a mere skeleton with wild dark hollows for eyes. A tattered prison uniform hangs in shreds from its frame. The apparition comes with a painful limp and a loud clatter. A tin can hanging about its waist makes an awful din every time the figure takes another step.

When it reaches the fence, the figure stops clumsily and positions itself a few steps from us. From such close proximity we can see the face clearly. It is the face of a skeleton with parchment-like skin covered with patches of light fuzz, and scabs. There are severe bruises on the high cheekbones. It's a face unlike anything I have ever seen. It resembles faces in the science-fiction magazines my brother Bubi used to read.

As the apparition stands there silently staring at us, a horrible certainty grips my insides. 'Bubi!' It is he. I know it.

Mummy's eyes open wide with horror. 'This is not he. This is not Bubi.'

Bubi's eyes focus on the piece of bread in Mummy's hand. His voice is an unearthly gasp, 'You may throw the bread over the fence, Mummy. The guard does not mind.'

Mummy's shriek is a bloodcurdling howl.

'Bubi! Is it you? Oh, God, is it really you?'

'Mummy, throw the bread over the fence.'

Mummy swallows hard. She swings her arm, and the soggy piece of bread flies above the barbed wire and lands in a puddle at Bubi's feet. With the deliberate, jerky motions of a robot, Bubi bends over to pick it up but stumbles and, with an ear-shattering clatter, rolls into the mud. Mummy gasps. I grasp her shoulder to give her support but cannot control my violent trembling.

We watch aghast as Bubi scrambles to his feet and, bread in hand, trudges away, clumps of mud tumbling from his tatters.

We wait. But he does not turn round. He keeps limping on, and soon his figure is swallowed by the twilight. But the clatter of his tin can continues to echo in the fog.

It reverberates in my being all night long.

TO FACE THE WORLD

WALDLAGER, APRIL 1945

Mummy is assigned to the kitchen brigade. She sits in an elongated block among many other women and peels potatoes from early morning till late at night. The peelers are permitted to eat from the potatoes. Sometimes they peel carrots, and they are permitted to eat from the carrots, too. But they are not permitted to take anything out of the kitchen – they are frisked every evening as they leave for the bunkers. A few days ago, a young girl from our transport was hanged in the *Appellplatz*, the central square of Waldlager, because at frisking time they found on her a carrot and two potatoes. Mummy does not dare hide any vegetable on her body, and I am glad.

Members of the kitchen brigade do not get any bread ration in order to compensate for the vegetables they eat during peeling. So now Mummy and I have only one bread ration among us. Until now Mummy and I shared one bread ration, and the other we threw over the barbed-wire fence for Bubi. Every evening after *Zählappell* we would watch Bubi as he hobbled to the fence with his clattering tin can and wait for the piece of bread to land on his side. Then he would retrieve the bread from the ground with great effort, and limp away, just as he came, without speaking.

Now I alone meet Bubi at the fence, because the kitchen brigade works late into the night, but Bubi takes no notice of the change. He continues his robotlike routine. I no longer attempt to speak to him; I have resigned myself to his silence. But tonight, before his departure, Bubi raises his eyes to mine, and slowly, haltingly begins to speak. 'Where is Mummy?' he asks.

The shock of Bubi's voice stuns me into momentary silence. This is the first time he has spoken since our arrival, almost two weeks ago.

'Where is Mummy, sis?' he repeats, and the unexpected thrill of hearing the familiar reference to myself nearly causes me to faint. I quickly pull myself together.

'Mummy works in the kitchen.'

'That's good. This way she can eat potatoes.' Then Bubi adds that he has been feeling much stronger. The bread ration he has received from us has made a significant difference to his condition.

I am bubbling with joy as I report this to Mummy in our bunker at night. Thank God, Bubi's health is improving. And he is OK mentally: he knows who we are. And his speech is not impaired. Our fears about Bubi were unfounded.

Mummy and I can barely sleep with the emotion of this new development. Our hopes are rekindled. Bubi will make it.

A few days later sudden, unexpected changes occur. The camp is agog with the news: the Americans are approaching, and Germans are surrendering the area without a fight. Mummy has just left for work, and I run to the fence to send a message to Bubi. As I emerge from our bunker, I run into a male inmate. A male inmate! From the men's camp beyond the barbed-wire fence!

'How did you get here?' I shout, and my head is reeling from the implications of his presence here.

'The gates are open,' he shouts back.

'Where are the guards?'

'There are no guards at the inner gates. Only at the main gate of the camp . . .'

I continue running towards the gate of the men's camp. Before I reach the gate I see Bubi coming towards me. I reach him and throw my arms about him. He, too, encloses me in his frail arms, and we stand there in a silent, timeless embrace. I close my eyes. Freedom. It has come. It has come.

Together we walk to our bunker and sit on its roof, a small grassy elevation. A soft breeze ruffles the tall grass around the bunker.

'So this is it,' I say with a deep intake of breath. 'Freedom. It has come.'

'Not yet. These are only rumours. We are not liberated yet,' Bubi warns.

'But where are the guards? Aren't you here, in our camp? The gates are open. Doesn't that mean everything? We are free to move about. The Americans will get here soon, and then we'll be liberated. But it has already begun . . .'

'One never can tell. One never can tell what the Germans will do next. There may be some fighting. The Americans aren't here yet . . .'

I cannot keep from talking about the future. 'After liberation I want to travel throughout Germany to find all our relatives in the different concentration camps, in different parts of the country. Especially Auschwitz. Most of them had arrived in Auschwitz. Daddy, we have no idea where he can be. He had been taken to a labour camp in Hungary; he is probably going to be liberated there. He will probably be the first to get home. Perhaps we should go home first. We will find everybody at home. Perhaps that's the best plan. To go home, and not waste time searching here in Germany, when everybody will be heading home anyway . . .'

Bubi interrupts. His voice is a low murmur. 'Whom do you expect to find?'

'Why, everybody. Daddy, Aunt Serena, Aunt Celia, Uncle Márton, Imre, Uncle Samuel, Aunt Regina, Grandmother, Suri, Hindi . . .'

Bubi raises his bony hand and places it slowly, hesitantly on mine. 'Look at me, Elli.' He searches my face, and I see infinite pain in his blue eyes. 'Look at me, Elli.' He touches my face ever so lightly, as he says slowly, very slowly, 'You will find no one. No one survived the death camps.'

His soft, tired voice drops even lower as he continues. 'We. We survived. We are the only ones. We are here. We are the only survivors.'

'But there are many other camps. Maybe they are there. Daddy, and Aunt Serena, and the others . . .'

'Daddy is different. He's a young man, he may have survived in the labour camp. He may be alive. He's the only one who had a chance. He's strong, athletic . . . But the others, don't expect to meet any of the others.'

'You mean, Aunt Serena? But she was taken to a camp for older people.'

'There is no such camp. Aunt Serena was taken to the gas chamber.'

'That's a lie! A lie they were telling us in Plaszow. They told you a lie. You know it's a lie!'

'You know it's not a lie . . . I had friends who worked in the *Sonderkommando*. I know all the details.'

'What details?'

'The *Sonderkommando* was a special unit. It was they who removed the bodies from the gas chambers. It was their job to strip the bodies of all valuables, even gold teeth, even teeth with gold fillings . . . before putting them into the ovens.' Bubi's voice lowered to a whisper. 'Sometimes they recognized the bodies . . . Younger siblings, parents, close relatives . . . Elli, all children, and adults older than forty-five . . . went to the gas.'

'Little Andy, Elizabeth, Uncle Samuel, Aunt Regina, Grandmother . . .?'

He nods. 'They all went to the gas chambers.'

'My God! It can't be true . . . Aunt Celia, we met Aunt Celia in Auschwitz. And Hindi. And Suri.'

'If you met then, they made the first selection – they may be alive. But since then so many have died. Do you know how many died here during the winter? And how many are dying daily? Every morning at *Zählappell* we find friends missing. The *Blockälteste* orders two men to go into the bunker and carry out those who died during the night. The corpses are placed on the lines and counted in the *Zählappell* until they are officially reported dead to the authorities.'

I sit stunned. Shattered. We are the survivors. Perhaps there is no one else. Only the three of us.

I had known about the gas chambers all along. The shadow of the gas chambers followed us even when we left Auschwitz. And yet, I had stubbornly clung to the myth of the camp for the children and the elderly. Some children must have survived.

'No. No children survived. They were all gassed.'

'And the mothers? The mothers were with the children. I saw the mothers go together with the children, to the other side. What happened to the mothers?'

'Mothers were gassed together with their children.'

'No, Bubi. Do not say that! Do not say that!'

We sit silently for a long time on the green slope that forms the roof of the bunker. The tall grass continues to sway and shudder in the cool April wind. Freedom. The Americans will be here soon, and we will be liberated. We will be freed – to do what? To face a world in which little children were gassed with their mothers. To face the world in which this was possible.

My God. My God. I have just been robbed of my freedom.

The Lost Game

IN THE TRAIN, 23–27 APRIL 1945

It is Tuesday morning, the last week of April 1945. At *Zählappell* open trucks arrive in the square. In quick order we are loaded on to trucks and driven out of the camp to the train station. Mühldorf station. Thousands of striped male uniforms, thousands of grey women's uniforms pour from hundreds of trucks straight on to hundreds of wagons. One hundred to a wagon. A sea of prison population is being shipped away from the approaching liberation.

Where are they taking us? Rumours circulate. We are being shipped to a long, deep tunnel where we will be blown to bits. The Germans prefer no witnesses to their atrocities. So we are to be liquidated in the trains.

Only rumours. Pay no attention to them. We have survived until now despite rumours. The Americans are near, the Germans would not dare kill us now, so near the end. God, do not let the rumours be right.

Where can Bubi be? I was going to meet him after *Zählappell*, as we had every day since the gates between our camps were opened. Where is he now? Is he among this sea of blue stripes being loaded on to the train? By nightfall the loading ends and the train begins to roll.

The wagon is jammed to capacity. There is a small window laced with metal bars near the corner where Mummy and I are crouching, and I can see the lovely woods we are leaving. A cool April breeze rushes in through the small window and we drink in the fresh air with mouths wide open. Now the train goes round a bend and I can see as far as the engine. Incredible! There are at least one hundred wagons between us and the engine! As I look the other way, I can see perhaps even more. My God. I have never seen such a chain of wagons, over two hundred! Where are they shipping so many prison inmates, one hundred to a wagon? Where can they house so many? They are evacuating the camps to escape the enemy closing in on all sides. The circle is getting smaller. Where will they find room for us? God, help us. Do not let the rumours be true.

The train rolls slowly all night, all day. Again all night, and all day. No food or drink. How could they feed all this multitude? Tens of thousands. For days before evacuation we barely received any food. On Thursday we stand in a forest clearing for hours on end.

From my corner perch I am watching a dogfight involving three fighter planes. One plane is hit and bursts into flames, and is now careening in a wide, flaming arc behind the trees. There is a series of loud explosions somewhere beyond my vision.

Now we move rapidly through deep forests and rolling hills and long, dark tunnels. And then slowly, in spurts, among budding fields and sprawling villages, little roadside inns and distant towns. We roll in and out of stations. Sometimes we stand for hours at a station, and sometimes we pass one without pause. And through it all, nagging hunger and thirst in the wagon.

By Friday morning I am not hungry any more. The violent hunger pangs have mellowed into a dull, persistent ache. An obliging lightheadedness lulls me into an apathetic numbness. Mummy also sleeps for longer periods. Her nagging hunger must have subsided somewhat. Brilliant sunshine filters through the cracks of the wagon. The train is standing still.

We must have been standing for a long, long time; my recollection of the train's movement is distant. I prop myself up on my elbows with extreme effort. My fellow passengers are sprawled on each other in a stupor. Mummy is also in deep sleep; her head is rolled on my left shoulder. I ease it slowly, gently aside and rise to my feet to get a view through the small window.

The train is perched on a high embankment above a softly sloping valley and a wide-open green cornfield. I can see houses in the distance, a small hamlet. High hills loom on the horizon, dark, beautiful, and forbidding.

The entire foreground is flushed with bright sunshine; a playful gust ruffles the green sea of corn stalks. It is a gay, light-hearted spring day out there. In the wagon it is airless and dark, and the scent of apathy is suffocating. I sink back on to the floor in my corner and place Mummy's drooping head on my shoulder. How much longer will we stand still in this place?

Now it must be noon: the sun is high in the sky. Friday noon. We have been locked in here since early Tuesday morning. Without food. Or water. That makes this the fourth day without food. How long can a person survive without food? I do not remember learning anything about this at school. How much longer will we stand in one place? Who knows? I cannot bear standing still. It is easier to bear all this when we are moving. There is hope in movement. Motion means life. It's insufferable just to stand in one place, aimlessly, endlessly . . . locked in, crowded, thirsty, suffocating from lack of air. Why are we standing here so long?

My shoulder is getting tired. I shift Mummy's head to my lower arm. It chafes. Her hair is very short, and the bristles are stiff and prickly. She opens her eyes.

'Why don't you sleep a little, Elli? Why don't you get a little rest? I'll sit upright so you can put your head on my lap. . . .'

All at once, the doors are wrenched open, and cold air rushes into the wagon. Two men in striped uniforms leap into the car shouting, 'We are free! We are free! Get out of the wagon!'

The chill gust and noise shake everyone awake from the lethargic daze. 'What's happening? What's going on? What's going on?' We all scramble to our feet and surge towards the wide-open door. Drunk with the sudden onrush of fresh air, we lumber down the metal steps. The wagon is empty within moments.

Out on the platform, the air is filled with the roar of thousands pouring out of the wagons, scampering down on the high embankment, and shouting, cheering, howling, whooping with ecstasy. The entire valley is filled with a swarming multitude of striped prison uniforms, grey prison dresses. The narrow embankment is also covered with men and women laughing, and crying, and embracing everyone they meet, or just aimlessly milling about among the tracks. 'We are free! We are free!'

Most inmates head for the green cornfield. Hundreds are tearing at green husks of corn and eating them. Others are devouring the young leaves. And some are heading towards the hamlet in the distance. But where are the Americans? Or the Germans? Only inmates are to be seen everywhere.

'Mummy, let's go to the cornfield. We will pick some corn. Or we will go to the village to get some food there. Everyone is going.'

'I'm not going from here until we find Bubi. He must be in this transport. We must find him.'

'How can we find him? That's impossible. There are thousands and thousands of people dispersed in every direction. He might have gone to the fields. Or to the village. We will never find him here at the train.'

'I'm not going anywhere until we find him!' Mummy's despair spills over into fury and panic. 'I'm not going anywhere!' Then, having spent the last ounce of her energy in her angry outburst, she continues in a low, tired voice, 'He could not go to the fields. He could not even get off this steep embankment. He has no strength to walk even . . . He must be here somewhere among the wagons. Or maybe he is in one of them. He might have been too weak to get off. He may just be helplessly lying there, in one of the abandoned wagons.'

We start on a long trek along the endless row of wagons, and peer into each. Most are not empty. There are men and women lying about in the dark interiors, and we call to them, asking about Bubi. Not one of them answers. Are they asleep? Are they dead? Should we climb into each wagon to see if any of them is Bubi . . .?

But Mummy trudges on, and I follow. There are many others who, like us, simply plod along the tracks. But they do not seem to be looking for anyone. They are simply walking about in a daze. We address these walkers, we inquire about Bubi, but they do not answer. They do not seem to hear.

Many lie on the ground, on the tracks, on the metal steps leading to the wagons. They seem unaware of what is going on all about them. Mummy and I crash ahead, from one wagon to another, in a futile search for my brother. The bulk of the prisoners have left the embankment. The valley is covered with a carpet of prison stripes.

'Mummy, there is no point in hanging about here. This train is endless. We cannot look into every single wagon. Let's go and try and get some food . . .'

'I'm not leaving until we find Bubi. I'm not leaving until we find Bubi. I'm not leaving until . . . Bubi!'

He is limping towards us, slowly, deliberately dragging his tattered, injured leg.

'Bubi!' I cannot believe my eyes. How can this happen? Among the thousands, we meet face to face. He, too, was looking for us near the train.

Bubi is in very poor condition. He is barely breathing. His wound has opened and blood is trickling down his leg. His face is badly bruised from a brutal kick he had received. Who kicked him in the face? When? He cannot remember.

The three of us sit on the embankment, and all around us inmates are disappearing. We are almost alone.

Suddenly, there is the sound of rapid gunfire. Another volley, now louder. Squirts of red slash the green valley. Shrieks of pain and panic are interspersed with rounds of shooting. Inmates are dropping among the cornstalks like toy tin soldiers, and their bodies rapidly form large red piles among the green corn.

'Zurück in die Waggons!' Back into the wagons. 'Los! Los!' Orders shouted in hysterical German accompany incessant gunfire, and the multitude, like a giant torrent, surges towards the embankment. The shooting continues, and the mad, upward rush is intermittently blocked by the bodies rolling downward among the ranks. 'Back into the wagons!'

What happened? Where are the Americans?

Within minutes the embankment is swarming with inmates – many bleeding from heads, shoulders, abdomens, limbs – running, limping, tottering towards the wagons.

Mummy, Bubi and I scramble to our feet and hurry towards the nearest wagon in the segment reserved for women. Mummy tears a piece off her skirt, and ties the cloth about Bubi's head as if it were a kerchief. 'Here. You are a woman now. No one will notice the difference. I want you to come into our wagon. I will take care of you.'

In the insane rush no one pays heed, and before the wagon fills to capacity, the doors are slammed shut from the outside, and the train begins to roll immediately. The sun is setting. From the small, barred window I can see the green valley studded with pools of red, and hundreds of prone bodies in striped uniform. The train picks up speed and rolls past the valley of the dead and the dying.

Where to?

What happened to our liberation? Why are we back again in a German prison truck? Are we being herded like cattle to slaughter? Is this all a game? A sinister, cruel diversion?

My God, is it our destiny to be pawns in a game? When will the game be over?

Once again we are prisoners locked behind bars, still hungry, thirsty, dazed. And very tired.

Except those who are lying dead in the cornfield. For them the game is over. Their bid for freedom was silenced suddenly, arbitrarily. Have they lost the game?

Or have we?

IT's an American Plane!

IN THE TRAIN, 28 APRIL 1945

The train keeps rolling among high mountains and dark forests. Mummy and I huddle together, hoping with our mutual body heat to form a shield of protection against the bitter cold in the wagon. Bubi is lying on his back with closed eyes, motionless. He is still alive. His breath is an uneven series of faint eruptions through partially opened lips.

No one speaks. There are no words for the events of yesterday, the sudden bliss of liberty, the brief, intoxicating gasps of freedom, the sudden reversal, the shooting, the bloody corpses in the cornfield. . . . And the prison train half full with wounded, starved, and apathetic inmates rattles on and on.

Faint rays of early dawn filter through the cracks of the cattle truck. The heads of prone bodies bounce and bob in tune with the steady jolt of the train's clank and clatter. Only a few feeble cries of pain and muffled groans disrupt the silence of apathy and the rhythm of the moving train.

By noon we reach a station, and the train stops. The cessation of movement awakens its inhabitants. One by one they stir and scramble into a sitting position. But Bubi remains still.

Mummy crawls to him and strokes his face. 'Bubi. Do you hear me? Can you hear me?'

He opens his eyes. 'I'm dizzy,' he says, and shuts his eyes again.

There is a loud shouting outside. One of the girls crawls over to the window and peers out.

'I see white trucks with large red crosses . . . many German soldiers.' Her voice is a croak.

The Red Cross. Perhaps they came to take the wounded.

The loud shouting continues. Finally we make out the words in German: 'All line up near your window! Hold your dish out! The Red Cross is handing out warm soup. One by one, step to the window, and reach out with your dish!'

Soup! Warm soup! In a second the bedraggled prisoners crowd near the window. I untie my dish from about my waist and with great effort get to my feet. The wagon is spinning about me. Mummy is helping Bubi to his feet, but he keeps tripping and falling. She tries to prop him up, but both tumble to the floor. Holding on to the wall I make my way towards them. I manage to reach them, and the two of us pull Bubi to his feet. Supporting him on two sides, the three of us inch our way to the window.

By the time we reach the window, the crowd dwindles. Many are sitting and slurping the steaming yellow liquid. The soup's aroma saturates the wagon and makes my body tremble. It's our turn. Mummy supports Bubi with both hands as he approaches the window and reaches out with his right hand holding the dish. I am supporting Mummy from behind.

There is a burst of machine-gun fire. A sudden impact hurls Bubi backwards against Mummy and both fall to the floor, blood spurting from Bubi's forehead. The dish in Bubi's hand is covered with blood. *Rat-tat-tat-tat* . . . machine-gun fire from every direction. Everyone about me falls to the floor. Blood is bubbling from the shoulder of the girl next to me. The girl on my other side tumbles face down, her soup spilled. A hole in the middle of her back is spurting blood like a fountain. As I lie flat on the floor I see streaks of fire darting through the walls from all sides, and zigzagging through the wagon. One such flash hits my neighbour in the face, and her eye splatters on her left cheek.

I cover my head with my tin dish. Whatever happens I must survive. Arms, legs don't matter. I must protect my head to survive.

'Mummy, put your dish over your head, and lie flat on the floor!' Mummy can't hear. Machine-gun fire drowns out my voice. I scream with all my might, 'Mummy, put your dish over your head! Lie flat, Mummy!'

Mummy does not hear. She is holding Bubi's bleeding head in her lap and bandaging it with a piece of cloth she has torn from her dress. I shriek hysterically, 'Mummy! Leave him alone! He was hit in the head. You can't help him! Lie flat so you don't get killed also . . . Mummy, please, please, don't get killed.'

I know this is the end. Yet somehow, somehow I must survive. Even though around me everyone is dying, I want to stay alive. Panic paralyses me into one obsessive thought: to live. To live!

The Red Cross food trucks were a Nazi trap: they lined us up at the window with the ruse of the warm soup distribution in order to hit us more easily with machine-gun fire. I know this is the end. They will keep shooting until everyone in the wagon is dead. Yet somehow I must stay alive. I must. I must live.

Mummy cradles Bubi's head, unaware of the relentless barrage of gunfire. She is oblivious to death and danger about her. A young girl's leg is torn off at the knee, and she sits holding the lower leg. When she lets go, the lower leg falls to the floor and she stares at the knee bone, a bloody stump protruding from the tattered thigh. Then she begins to scream.

She is Lilli, the pretty sixteen-year-old girl who entertained us with her singing in Augsburg. I idolized her: she was everything I was not – petite, brunette, a talented singer. I grab her lower leg, and with my two hands press it against the bloody knee stump. It is still attached by a shred of skin.

'Hold it!' I scream at Lilli and wait for her to place her two hands on the bloody limb before taking mine away. 'Hold it!' Lilli stops screaming and obeys my insane impulse, believing that by pressing the parts against each other they will grow together again. She holds the leg, her hands overflowing with blood.

The shooting has stopped. A sudden deadly silence. We look at each other. Did the shooting really stop? Is it all over? And we are not all dead. Eight dead. Many wounded. Some were not hit at all. Mummy and I are covered in blood, but neither of us was hit. Bubi lies unconscious but he's alive: he is breathing, but blood is seeping through the rag Mummy tied about his head. He is also bleeding at the right elbow.

Lilli is sitting in a pool of blood, trembling violently but still holding on to her leg. She does not answer when I ask her if she is in pain. The girl whose eye was shot out complains of a headache. She does not seem to realize that she lost an eye.

The youngest of the three Stadler sisters from a neighbouring town in Czechoslovakia is bleeding profusely from one arm, and complains of severe pain. Her elder sister, a tall girl with a lame leg, keeps soothing her with endearments. Both seem unaware of their eldest sister's condition. She is lying next to me near the wall, face down, the hole in the middle of her back oozing dark blood. She is a teacher, and once she substituted for our teacher in Somorja. I liked her better than our teacher and I told her so in Augsburg. This made her happy, and from then on she gave me a smile every time we passed each other. I bend over her. I cannot hear her breathing. I touch her arm. It is cold.

All at once the wagon doors slide open. German soldiers shout at us from the doorway to get out of the wagon. The enemy planes are expected to stage another attack. We are permitted to leave the wagons and hide in the forest. *Los!* Move!

Some start to crawl towards the door. But most are unable to move. '*Los!* Move! The planes are coming!' This must be another trap. But I see German soldiers running up on an incline towards the nearby forest.

'Elli, you go. I cannot move. I'm staying here with Bubi.'

'Mummy, you must. You can make it.'

'And what about Bubi? We cannot leave him here.'

I know Bubi is beyond help. I have not heard him breathe for some time now. But I do not want to leave Mummy behind.

'Let's take him along.' I crawl over and lift Bubi by the shoulders. Without protesting Mummy lifts his legs, and we drag him towards the door. All at once he opens his eyes. I scream: 'Mummy, Bubi is alive!'

'Of course he is alive. You didn't know?'

I didn't know. How wrong I was! He is alive. Oh, my God. I start to weep and my tears are dripping on Bubi's head as I drag him by the shoulders. At the door I prop Bubi up in a sitting position, climb off the wagon, and help Mummy down. Once outside, she collapses on the ground.

'I can climb off if you help me,' Bubi mutters. I help him crawl off the wagon, and he is leaning on my shoulder as I pull Mummy to her feet. People ahead are crawling up on the green incline towards the forest. Holding on to each other, the three of us start crossing a gravelly strip flanking the tracks. But there is a wire running horizontally about a foot high in the air, and neither Bubi nor Mummy are able to step over it. They cannot lift their feet high enough. I bend down to lift Bubi's foot, but he loses his balance, and all three of us tumble on to the tracks.

Mummy cries, 'It's no use. I cannot go on. Elli, you go ahead. Leave us here.'

There is a low steady hum of approaching planes. They are back.

'Let's crawl under the wagons.'

The three of us crawl under a truck on all fours. A few other inmates are also there. Beth Stadler and her injured sister are lying on their bellies. The planes are flying low. A plane dives down into a clearing at the edge of the forest some hundred yards ahead and sprays machine-gun fire into a cluster of inmates and German soldiers among the trees. It's an American plane!

Incredible. An American plane! So it is true: it is an 'enemy' attack. But why would American planes fire at a transport of concentration-camp inmates? Can't they see the striped uniforms? And why would the Germans attempt to save us?

The planes fly overhead, spray machine-gun fire in every

direction, and fly off. Within minutes, they return, fly low, and attack a third time.

The noise of the planes' engines combined with the sound of rapid machine-gun fire is ear-shattering. I can see bluish flashes zigzagging in every direction. An aeroplane is diving towards the trains. Eva, a co-worker from Augsburg who is crouching on my right, is hit and killed instantly. Beth Stadler lies on top of her younger sister, and whispers, 'Don't worry, little sis, I will not let them hurt you this time. I'm covering you with my own body. If they shoot here, it's I who will be hit, not you.'

Her sister does not answer. She is dead. She's been hit in the side of the neck.

Beth Stadler goes wild. She crawls out from under the wagon and positions herself out in the open. She turns her face upward, waves her arms at the sky, and howls, 'God! Do you see me? I am here! Kill me! Kill me! You killed my two sisters. My two beautiful, talented sisters. And you spared me, a cripple. Why didn't you spare them? Why didn't you kill me instead? Kill me now! I don't want to live. What will I tell my parents? What will I tell my mother? Oh, God, what will I tell her?'

The planes drone overhead. Mummy calls to her, 'Beth, come here. Come under the wagon fast.'

In a daze Beth turns around, and crawls towards Mummy. Then she crawls over to her dead sister, embraces her and begins to sob.

The planes are gone. We continue crouching under the wagons, waiting in silence. But they do not return. Beth's sobs break the silence. 'What will I tell my parents? The cripple survived. And my two beautiful, talented sisters are dead!' We crouch silently, waiting. The planes do not return. The attack is over. The German guards and the inmates start to emerge from the forest. We, too, crawl out from under the wagons. Beth is dragging the body of her sister.

'Back into the wagons!'

Beth carries her sister on her shoulder into the wagon. Mummy and Bubi and I support each other as we clamber back into the wagon. Beth lays her sister alongside the older one who is face down near the wall. The wounded lie quietly. Several are no longer breathing. The girl shot in the eye is also dead.

The wagon floor is covered with pools of blood. The three of us find a dry corner. Lilli lies in a stupor, trembling violently, her leg still hanging on a shred of skin. She is no longer holding on to it.

Two guards appear in the open doorway. 'Are there any corpses in here?'

'Yes, there are.'

'How many?'

We count. 'Twelve.'

Two males in bloody, striped uniforms clamber into the car, carry out the dead bodies one by one, and place them on the strip of gravel alongside the tracks. Despite Beth Stadler's pleas, her two sisters are also carried out of the wagon and placed on the heap of bodies opposite the open doors of our truck.

The sun is setting by the time the train begins to pull out. The doors are left open, and Beth stands in the truck's entrance staring at her sisters' bodies as the train rolls past them with increasing speed and clatter.

'Remember, Beth,' Mummy reminds her, 'the anniversary of your sisters' deaths according to the Hebrew calendar is

three days before Lag B'Omer. Your sisters' *Yahrzeit* is the thir-
tieth day of Omer.'

I look at Mummy in amazement. How can she have her wits
about her at such moments? How can she remember the
Hebrew date after what we've just been through? How can she
think of *Yahrzeits*?

The train picks up speed. It is getting dark. Sabbath is coming to a close. It is 28 April 1945.

FREEDOM, AT LAST

SEESHAUPT, 30 APRIL 1945

Perhaps our guards no longer care whether we escape or not. The doors of the wagon stand wide open. It is bitter cold inside it. Most of us are wounded, some critically. The others are too weak to move.

We roll with a steady, loud clatter amid high mountains and deep forests. The train moves on all day. All night. We have been in the cattle truck a whole week, without food, without water. The night seems endless. The rattle of the train goes on for ever.

Lakes glisten with eerie grey light. There is deadly silence in the wagon. My brother is lying with closed eyes, his head in Mummy's lap. Mummy sits propped against the wall in the corner, her head hanging to one side, her eyes half closed, her mouth wide open. I know she's asleep.

Lilli is silent now. She stopped whimpering some time ago. I touch her. She is very hot.

Beth is silent, too. She's not asleep, though. She leans against the wall quite upright, staring ahead. Her eyes seem enormous in the shadowy darkness of the car.

The two remaining sisters from the small Hungarian village huddle together, asleep. Judy, the girl from Budapest with the injured shoulder, also sits upright, and seems wide awake. She wheezes very loudly, the only human sound in the wagon. Sometimes she gasps for air, and then Mummy trembles in her sleep, raises her head and opens her eyes for a second, then closes them and lets her head fall to one side again. Judy must have been shot in the lungs. That is why she has trouble breathing. I hope we will be liberated soon. She needs urgent medical attention.

The two cousins, Irene and Martha, are lying near me, asleep. Irene was injured in the face and Martha bandaged her wound with the cherished scarf she had received from her father across the barbed wire in Dachau. The scarf was Martha's talisman, and now it is a blood-stained wrapping on her cousin's face.

Suddenly, Irene grows restless. She lifts her head and rips the scarf off her face. She sits up abruptly and shrieks, 'Martha! I can't see! I can't see anything!'

Martha awakens. 'Don't take off the bandage. Your face is still bleeding.'

'But I can't see! The bandage is off and I can't see anything! I'm blind! Martha, I'm blind! My God, I'm blind! I'm blind! I'm blind!'

Her screams wake the wagon. Words of comfort emerge from every corner. It's dark in the car; no one can see. Your blindness may be temporary, caused by the sudden flash you saw. You lost too much blood; your lack of vision is a sign of weakness. Your face and eyelids are swollen, blocking your sight. Finally Irene quietens down and all sink again into lethargic silence.

But Irene does not rest. She launches into a low-pitched monologue describing every detail of the machine-gun barrage on the wagon . . . the blinding flash which hurled her to the ground and caused her to bleed profusely, the pain, the noise, the blood, the blood. . . . With each repetition her voice grows more hoarse. Her words begin to slur. Her sentences crumble into phrases, disjointed, confused. But she talks on, incessantly, feverishly.

Martha attempts to quiet her, to no avail. Irene is beyond hearing. I touch her gesticulating arm. It is very hot.

Irene no longer describes the carnage caused by the strafing attack. She is talking about her family now, her hometown in Czechoslovakia, her mother, her father . . . her sisters.

Pale light filters into the wagon. I look at Irene's face. Two empty eye sockets stare back at me. I cover my face with both hands. God! Oh, God! God!

Irene grabs my arm. 'Look there! Do you see it? What a beautiful meadow! Beautiful! Do you see it? There! There!'

She gesticulates wildly. She points at the dark wall of the wagon. 'There! Beautiful meadow . . . trees, birds . . . beautiful . . .'

Then she falls silent.

Now Lilli begins to whimper again. 'Are you in pain?' I ask, but she does not respond. Her lips are dry. Her leg stump is no longer bleeding.

'Water . . .' she whispers, in a barely audible tone.

With the brightening light I see she is very pale. I touch her brow. It is cool. I stroke her face gently. I have no strength to cry. I have no tears, no tears at all. Yet I hold a sob deep within. Not in my mind. My mind is blank. In my stomach. I'm sobbing in my stomach as I am stroking the cooling forehead of pretty little Lilli lying next to the ravaged face of gentle Irene.

'Mummy,' Lilli whispers. 'Mummy . . .' Her head hits the

floor of the wagon with a thump. She is dead.

During the morning hours Irene dies, too.

The train rolls on. All day. All night.

The first flickers of dawn pierce the car, and I realize that we have been standing for some time. I must have dozed off after all. In the cattle truck everyone is asleep, the dead and the living dead.

Judy is no longer wheezing, no longer gasping for air. The blood on the floor of the wagon has long dried.

Where are we? I want to peer between the slats but I cannot move. My limbs seem frozen. Better lie still and wait. Wait for the train to move again. Wait for the familiar rattle, which has become the only rhythm of life.

Slowly, eyes open all around. No one moves. No one breaks the numb compulsion of motionlessness. We lie still and wait.

In mid-morning sounds reach us. Human voices.

A shadow is cast into the wagon. Then another. The voices seem quite near now. With effort, I lift my head.

Two tall men in strange uniforms stand in the doorway. They look at us with a curious expression. One of them shakes his head and says something to the other. I do not understand what he says. I am very tired. It is difficult to concentrate. Then the two tall men in the strange uniforms leave the wagon.

In a few minutes a heavy-set officer with reddish cheeks appears. He speaks very loud in a strange Yiddish. 'Who are you? Are you Jews?' Then he repeats, 'Who are you? Do you understand me? Can you hear me? Can you speak Yiddish? Who can understand me?'

We all stare without answering. Finally Martha, nearest to the entrance, whispers, 'Who are you?'

'We are Americans. But who are you? Are you Jews? Are you men or women?'

'Americans?'

We all struggle into a sitting position. 'Americans!' So it has come. We are liberated. It is all over. We are free. The Americans have finally come. We are free. They've come at last. At last.

'Are you really American? Where are the Germans?'

'The Germans surrendered. We've arrested your guards. But who are you? What prison camp do you come from? Are you men or women?'

'We are Jewish women from the concentration camp at Dachau. We are unable to walk. Most of us are badly wounded . . . machine-gun fire. Two days ago this train was strafed by American fighter planes. There are many dead among us.'

'We've not eaten for many days. Many days,' I manage to speak. I am speaking German. The American seems to understand. 'We're very thirsty.'

'You'll get food soon. But first we must get you off the train. Can you get off the train?'

He gives me a hand, and helps me off the wagon. Then he helps Mother. Two German civilians carry my brother out of the wagon, and place him on the ground near the train tracks. They carry the bodies of Lilli, Irene, Judy and all the others out of the wagon, and place them beside the tracks. The entire station, every platform, is filled with the dead and wounded, and the living dead, all covered with blood. A sprawling horizontal multitude.

A large group of German civilians stands near the station house. They are the only vertical bodies. Except for the heavy-set American officer. He is making a speech to the 'Leading citizens of Seeshaupt . . .' Seeshaupt? That's a resort in Bavaria, an exclusive resort. 'Have you ever seen such horror? Such atrocities . . . maimed skeletons . . . Your government . . . your people bear responsibility . . .'

So this is it. Liberation. It's come. I am cold. The trembling in my stomach . . . Too much air . . . it's too light. I am very tired.

A middle-aged German woman approaches me. 'We didn't know anything. We had no idea. You must believe me. Did you have to work hard also?'

'Yes,' I whisper.

'At your age, it must've been difficult.'

At my age. What does she mean? 'We didn't get enough to eat. Because of starvation. Not because of my age.'

'I meant, it must have been harder for the older people.'

For older people? 'How old do you think I am?'

She looks at me uncertainly. 'Sixty? Sixty-two?'

'Sixty? I am fourteen. Fourteen years old.'

She gives a little shriek and makes the sign of the cross. In horror and disbelief she walks away, and joins the crowd of German civilians near the station house.

So this is liberation. It's come.

I am fourteen years old, and I have lived a thousand years.

I'm numb with cold. With hunger. With death and blood, and the rattle of the train rolling on and on. . . .

Freedom, at last.

Why don't I feel it? Why don't I feel it?

Homecoming

ŠAMORIN, JUNE 1945

The large military trucks are driven by handsome
young Americans with shiny black faces and quick
flashes of brilliant, white teeth. They must be good-
hearted men, these young black Americans – their
smiles give them away.

In the middle of June the 'repatriation' began.
Hundreds of thousands are waiting to leave the
refugee camps and return home. The first transports
went to various parts of Germany and Austria. And
now our turn has come: we are being 'repatriated' to
Czechoslovakia. Most of our friends are staying
behind. Their turn is next, transports to Hungary
and Romania.

We climb on to the huge military transport,
Mummy, Bubi and I, and are seated on metal planks
flanking the three sides of the open vehicle. Our new
belongings, a grey duffel bag and two smaller
bundles made of sheets and three green army blankets, are tossed on top of a luggage heap in the
middle of the truck.

Then, the roar of the engine, a sudden rush of open
air, frenzied waving, and we are off in twelve enormous, noisy vehicles. Very soon the transit camp

recedes into a bluish haze and the hills come racing to meet the curving road. We race ahead, suspended between sky and Bavarian Alps. Wide-open sky. Unbridled charge of savage wind. Freedom; exhilarating, intoxicating, threatening. I hold on to Bubi's arm with a firm grip. With eyes closed, chin raised, Bubi is thirstily drinking it all in through wide-open nostrils.

'Fast, isn't it?' My voice vibrates against the oncoming air current.

'Wonderful. Just wonderful. These black Americans, they call them Negroes, they are the best drivers in the world!'

'How do you know that?'

'I remember reading it somewhere.'

My brother Bubi knows everything. The road spirals upward on a narrow path. I'm not going to be afraid. I'm not going to be afraid.

The trucks race non-stop all night. Stars hang against a brilliant sky. The chill night air paralyses my body even under the blankets. My jaw is stiff from a thousand shivers. Aren't they ever going to stop? Don't they have to rest? They have been driving since yesterday morning.

'There are two of them. They are taking turns.'

By noon the next day the army vehicles come to a screeching halt in the centre square of a Gothic town. Thank God. Finally we can rest our weary limbs for a while here, I hope.

The drivers come to the back of the truck, and greet us with wan smiles. One of them says something in English, and then they begin to unload the luggage. With waves of their arms they indicate for us to get off the truck. We oblige, somewhat uncomprehending. As soon as the trucks are empty, the engines are revved up, and the vehicles take off in a cloud of exhaust fumes.

What's this? We stand, a lost bunch of worn travellers, in the midst of nowhere. Dusty cargo of the mighty American machines, we are dumped unceremoniously in the centre of a strange town. Where are we? What will become of us?

We find out that we are in Pilsen. Pilsen is Czechoslovakia. We are home. Our little crowd begins to scatter in every direction. Mummy, Bubi and I have to get to Bratislava in Slovakia, much father east, and the only transportation is by freight train. We head for the train station.

It is getting warm. Our duffel bag is much too heavy. Bubi and I are dragging it on rough roads, sweat soaking the new American army surplus clothes we received in the transit camp. With our free hands we are helping Mummy carry the smaller bundles.

At the station there is a freight train ready to leave for Bratislava tomorrow morning. The station master allows us to move into one of the trucks and spend the night. Mummy finds a wicker broom, and sweeps it clean. We spread our blankets, open our ration kit, and dine in the spacious luxury of an empty, cool wagon. What a stroke of good fortune!

By nightfall several other passengers find their way into our truck. They are all refugees of the war, heading home. Soon the wagon is full of people, and there is a pervading mood of expectation. For tomorrow.

It is noon when the wheels stir into motion and the truck begins to roll. We are moving at last.

Mountains mellow into rolling hills then flatten into wide-open stretches of green meadow. We are heading east towards the lowlands of the Danube Valley. The foliage is becoming familiar.

The train moves in sparse instalments, and it is only on the fourth day that we arrive at the outskirts of Bratislava. The train stops for several minutes, just long enough for the three of us to scamper off, dragging our bulky belongings. Our travelling companions wave frantically from the belly of the wagon as the train picks up speed and vanishes into the blinding sunshine.

Mummy, Bubi and I spend several days in Bratislava, until a farmer travelling east consents to give us a ride to our home town in his cart. It is called Šamorin now.

My first sight of Šamorin is obliterated by a hot summer haze and dust churned up by the horse's hoofs. The dull ache in my stomach changes to sharp stabs. The peasant cart turns the corner. There, on the small elevation of the deserted square, stands our house, now faded yellow with large patches of grey. A battered sign hangs above the shuttered shop front: FRIED-MANN – GENERAL STORE. The windows are dark. The gate is ajar.

'Here,' Mummy says. 'Stop here, please. And thank you kindly.'

The courtyard is deserted. The rooms are bare. The floors are covered with thick layers of dust. And something else. In the middle of every room there is a heap of human excrement.

Where is everything? The furniture, bedding, carpets, curtains, pots and pans. Even the pump from the well is gone. How will we get water?

And where is Daddy?

'Perhaps Daddy is staying with someone else. Until our return. He didn't want to be alone in this empty house. Soon we'll find out.'

Bubi limps into town to find out. I run over to our neighbours to borrow a broom. Mrs Plutzer stops in her tracks. 'Elli! Jesus Maria, it's Elli! You're back! Jesus is kind. You're alive.'

The Plutzers bring us a pitcher of milk, some eggs, and a bundle of straw to sleep on. We are home.

Thirty-two young boys and girls have returned. Our arrival makes the number thirty-five. Daddy has not come yet.

Then, one day, two weeks after our homecoming, Misi Lunger arrives and brings news about Daddy. He saw Daddy along the route home in the company of a man named Weiss from the village of Nagymagyar. What causes Daddy's delay? When news reaches us that Mr Weiss has arrived in his village, Bubi decides to go to Nagymagyar at once. A Šamorin cattle dealer on his way to some villages in the Nagymagyar vicinity offers Bubi a ride on his wagon early next dawn.

It is still dark when Bubi rises and takes off towards the home of the cattle dealer. I feel a tinge of regret that Mummy does not let me join my brother on the journey. It is a hazardous trip for a girl: the countryside is full of roaming Russian soldiers.

It's about 10 a.m. when Bubi, his face ashen, walks into the kitchen. 'Bubi, you're back so soon?'

'I did not go.'

'The cattle dealer did not go to Nagymagyar after all?'

'The cattle dealer went. I did not go.'

A cold hand stops the beating of my heart. Mummy looks intently into Bubi's eyes. Very, very quietly, she asks, 'Bubi, what happened?'

'We hung around for a long time before he was ready to start. When I climbed up next to him in the driver's seat, he said, "Look, kid. It's a shame you should make this long trip for nothing. The others told you to go to Nagymagyar because nobody wanted to be the one to tell you. I'm going to tell you the truth about your father. He's not coming home. He died in Bergen-Belsen two weeks before liberation. Lunger and Weiss buried him with their own hands." And so I did not go to Nagymagyar.'

Mummy freezes. I give a shriek and run into the yard. Bubi follows me.

'Come inside, Elli. There's the law. I have to rend a tear in your dress. And then we have to sit *shiva*.'

In the kitchen Mummy sits on the floor, staring into the vacuum.

'When news of the death reaches the family after the lapse of *shloshim*, the thirty-day mourning period, they sit *shiva* only for an hour, instead of a week,' Bubi explains, in a murmur. 'Daddy died in April, and now it's July.'

Bubi grips my collar to rend a tear in it, and I begin to howl like a wounded beast. Gently he pushes me down on the floor, and I sit *shiva* for Daddy.

There is nothing to keep us here any longer. Now we know that all the others are not coming home, either. News reaches us daily of family and friends who were taken to the gas, and others who died in one camp or another, or on the highways of Germany, on death marches. And others who died after liberation on their way home.

Each piece of news adds to a deepening sense of isolation. We are the only survivors, the three of us, just as Bubi said in Waldlager. There are no Jewish children here, no older people. The children I saw marching towards the smoke in Auschwitz, the little boy with the yellow clown, they were the last ones. When I see a child on the street, I see those children, and little Tommi, Susie and Frumet in the cattle truck heading for Auschwitz, and my insides turn numb with the pain of emptiness.

I want to go to Palestine, the Jewish Land, and live among people who share my inner voice. I want to hear the echo of that void reverberate in the voices of my fellow students, my fellow shoppers, my fellow pedestrians. When I reach for a bar of soap on the grocery shelf and my fingers cringe from the memory of soap made of 'pure Jewish fat', I want to glimpse the horror in the eyes of the next shopper reaching for a bar of soap. Can the void ever be filled?

Perhaps it can be shared. Perhaps in the Jewish Land.

But I have a problem. Bubi received an affidavit from a school in New York, and soon he will be leaving for America. The three of us had vowed never to be separated again. We must follow Bubi to America as soon as we can.

What's America like? Are there people in America who can understand? The compulsion to fill the void? The search, the reaching out? The sense of futility? The irrevocable statement that is Auschwitz? The loss of perspective? The total, irreconcilable loss?

Can anyone understand the pain of the uprooted? This was my home once, my town, my country. The pasture beyond our house was my childhood playground. The path leading to the Danube was *my* path. I can still hear Daddy's firm, light footsteps next to me in the grass as we hurry for a quick swim in our river. I can hear Mummy's cheerful chatter, Aunt Serena's soft singing far behind us. I can see Bubi and his friends striding ahead with fishing tackle, partially swallowed up by the tall grass. I can see the poplars swaying in the distance and the deep shady forest looming far beyond. I can smell the mist of the water, mingled with the odour of wet moss. I can hear the pealing of church bells and their echoes booming in the surrounding hills. It is all part of the fabric of my inner world – the Danube, the meadow, the Carpathian foothills and the town. Without it I am not whole. Yet it is no longer mine. It is not my home any more.

'America, Will You Be My Home?'

ŠAMORIN, AUTUMN 1945

It is a cloudless morning in autumn. The vibrancy of summer still shimmers in the air and paints splashes of sunshine across the rusty landscape.

I am back at school. I race down the street, inhaling all this beauty deep into my lungs with an intoxicating sense of freedom. Dare I run as fast as I please, and bask in this splendour without fear? Dare I enjoy the luxury of carrying notebooks under my arm, just like before? Sit in a classroom, among fellow students, just like before. Dare I feel like an adolescent – be silly and restless and indulgent and critical and boisterous and sentimental at will – just like my peers?

Dare I enjoy the luxury of being a girl? Having hair? Wearing a dress and underwear? And ordinary shoes, girls' shoes? Having a bar of soap and a toothbrush? And being noticed by boys?

As I run, two Russian soldiers approach and click their tongues. One attempts to block my path, but I swerve round with practised speed and cross the square at a trot.

A brilliant red star flutters above the entrance of the school building. No pupils are to be seen on the wide front stairs. Classes must have started. I have no watch; no way of telling the time. Whatever happened to the eight o'clock church bells?

The floor in my classroom still smells of stale oil, and the blackboard is cracked in the same places. The squeaking of chalk against the freshly washed board gives me goosebumps just like before. And the sound of the bell at the end of each session gives me a sudden start, just like before.

But everything else is different. My own class graduated while I was away, and the kids in this class are total strangers. They are children of ethnic Slovaks 'repatriated' by the government in a huge 'population transfer' from Hungary, beyond the Danube. Our town and the entire region became part of Czechoslovakia once again while I was away. Czech and Slovak teachers came in place of the Hungarian ones I knew and loved, and the language of instruction is Slovak. I do not see a single familiar face in school.

I had longed to see Mrs Kertész, our teacher. In the camps, in my mind and sometimes in my dreams, I wrote long, elaborate letters to her, describing all that was happening to me. I had imagined returning to school one day and handing her all the letters, like chapters in a book. I had imagined her comments and corrections, her smile, her praise. But she is gone, and no one in class has even heard of her.

I am the only one in the class who was born here, in this very town. Yet I am the only outsider. I do not belong to any group. The others have compatriots they know from 'the old country'. They came in groups from their native towns. The kids I grew up with are no longer here. My Gentile schoolmates were transferred to Hungary with their families. And my Jewish schoolmates? Almost all of them did not return from Auschwitz.

Thirty-six of us have returned. Thirty-two girls and boys, and four adults, of Šamorin's one hundred Jewish families. Thirty-six from over five hundred people – parents, siblings, grandparents, uncles, aunts and cousins, friends, neighbours, shopkeepers and teachers, toddlers and teenagers.

The thirty-six of us meet every day in the communal dining room we call *Tattersall*. *Tattersall* means racetrack in German. I don't know who gave this curious name to the abandoned building the authorities allocated for our use. The peculiar name stuck, and it became a metaphor for our exclusivity. The *Tattersall* – a small yard, a large kitchen and two empty rooms with coarse, unpainted tables and chairs – is our private cocoon. Here we eat together and carry on endless discussions. The past is too much with us, too raw. We do not speak about the past. Neither do we talk about the present: it simply does not exist. In the *Tattersall*, the future is the only reality. It is the only topic of discussion.

And the future lies far from our birthplace, the motherland that had brutally expelled us from its womb. Every one of us nurtures a fond dream of a distant land. For most, this land is Palestine, Eretz Yisrael. Most anticipate the day when their names on Jewish Agency lists will turn into permits for Palestine, and the transports will start. They live for the day, for the hour.

Others have relatives across the Atlantic – in America, Canada or South America – and they live in anticipation of documents. They dream of documents, talk of documents – letters of invitation from relatives, visas from consulates, exit permits.

We, too, mother, brother, and I, live on the emotional verge of departure. A few weeks ago a letter arrived from Daddy's younger brother in America, and it changed our lives. The letter was addressed to Daddy. 'Dear Brother,' it read. 'I saw your name on a list of survivors published in one of New York's Jewish newspapers, and I hasten to write, to communicate my great joy at the happy news. Please write to me as soon as you receive this letter, and let me know about the rest of the family. I want to help you to come to America. As soon as I receive your letter, I will start all the necessary procedures. Your loving brother.'

It was Mummy's sad duty to inform my uncle about the New York newspaper's tragic error. By return mail Daddy's brother offered to help us to get to America and find a new home in New York where he had made his home.

How ironic. Daddy's impossible dream would become our reality. He used to point at the tallest skyscraper on postcards from his brother. 'See?' he would say, 'over a hundred storeys high. Can you ever imagine a building over a hundred storeys high? This is Broadway,' he would point out. 'When we get to New York,' he promised with a smile, 'I will buy you the prettiest dress on Broadway.'

Oh, Daddy. I still see your tall, slim silhouette disappearing into the dawn. Will I ever stand at the foot of that skyscraper? Will I ever walk on Broadway, and buy a beautiful dress like you promised? Will your promise materialize in the future while you yourself have vanished for ever in the haze of the past?

Daddy, we found the small porch with our jewellery in the dark, musty earth of the cellar where you buried it. We dug twenty-five centimetres deep, just as you said, and there it was, the small, mouldy, cotton pouch. The jewellery is here, Daddy, but you are not.

Mummy sold some pieces of jewellery to the Russian soldiers to pay for Bubi's board in Bratislava. Since the beginning of the school year, Bubi has been living in the Slovakian capital, some twenty kilometres away, where he is enrolled in a preparatory course for graduation. It is a course designed for students who missed out on education because of the war. Bubi has gained some weight, and his leg wound has healed, and Mummy induced him to return to school. He cannot return to his former school in Budapest: the Hungarian capital is now beyond reach on the other side of a rather unfriendly border.

Mummy is busy sewing dresses for the Russian soldier girls, in exchange for eggs, flour, live chickens, even lightbulbs. Most of the shops are closed, and those that are open are empty. Even if there were merchandise, we could not buy it, as we have no money. It's a blessing that Mummy knows how to make dresses. How else would we live?

The Russian army personnel have everything. The young soldier girls bring pieces of fabulous fabrics and they are thrilled with the frilly blouses, colourful skirts, and fanciful dresses Mummy makes for them. Our house is always full of *barishnas*, and *tovarishes*, their male companions; five soldiers to every soldier girl. The *tovarishes* bring along their harmonicas and balalaikas, their good voices and their good humour. In conversation with them I practise the Russian I learn in school, and they love it. I'm Mummy's interpreter when taking orders for a new dress or bartering for the price. It's fun.

I love the Russians. They fought the Germans and helped to save our lives. That's why I love the language. Our neighbours, Slovaks and Hungarians alike, despite the Russians. They see them as the enemy. They see them as crude and primitive occupiers. But to me they are heroes.

Three weeks ago Bubi and I, while helping to clean the synagogue, found Hebrew and English textbooks in the rubble. So I began teaching myself Hebrew and English. I find English very easy because of its similarity to German. Hebrew is more difficult because of the different script. The printed Hebrew characters are familiar from the *siddur*, the prayer book, but the written script is new to me. And the language itself, the vocabulary and the grammar, is totally different from the other languages I know.

I think of my poems often. Sometimes I long to see them again, to read them again. Is Pista Szivos, the young Hungarian guard from the ghetto, still keeping my notebook and awaiting my return as he had vowed? His little village in Hungary is not very far from here. It's not more than sixty kilometres from the other side of the river. At times I dream of crossing my beloved Danube by boat, and retrieving the notebook that holds the secrets of my innermost self. But I have no right to such self-indulgence. My friends, my family, all those achingly dear to me, my entire world, rose up in smoke, vanished. How dare I retain such passion for my possession? Such urge for self-gratification? How dare I violate the agony of Auschwitz?

Now Mummy knows the secret of my notebook, and she reassures me, 'You'll see. One day the young Hungarian soldier will appear on our doorstep and return your poems.' But I resolved to relinquish my poems. And I resolved not to think about finding Pista Szivos in his small Hungarian village across the Danube. Neither did Pista Szivos ever try to find *me*. I wonder: Has he returned from the war? Or has he also become one of its casualties?

My relationship with Mummy has undergone a transformation. The unavoidable reversal of our roles in the camps after her accident changed her attitude towards me. Although once again she became the strong, no-nonsense yet sympathetic guiding hand, there is a striking difference. She treats me with respect, and frequently lavishes excessive praise on me. I am happy yet uncomfortable with Mummy's lavish praise.

Just now I desperately need Mummy's understanding and respect. Yesterday, when one of the boys told me of secret transports to Palestine, I was gripped by an overwhelming desire to join them. Suddenly I knew with unmistakable clarity that I did not want to go to America.

How can I tell Mummy and my brother that I do not want to go to America? The two people I love so, how can I tell them that my choice lies elsewhere? How can I tell them that since yesterday I have lost my yearning for America?

Mummy has just sat down at the kitchen table to write a letter to our uncle in America, and I know this is my chance to break my silence.

'Mummy, I must speak to you.'

Mummy raises her head but her mind still lingers on the letter's opening sentence. 'You wanted to say something?'

'Not just say something, Mummy. I must speak to you.'

'Now? Right now? I've just started this letter.'

'Yes.'

She puts down the pen, and I look straight into her eyes. 'Mummy, I'm not going to America.'

Her eyes widen, and her mouth opens a little.

'I want to go to Palestine.'

'Palestine . . .? Why Palestine?'

'Palestine, Eretz Yisrael, is part of us. That's where we belong. Mummy, can't you see? Can't you?'

Mummy forgets to close her mouth. Her eyes grow bluer than ever. I search them for hurt or anger but there is neither. There is only bafflement.

'Mummy, Eretz Yisrael is our only home. New York will not be home. We can make it in New York but it will never be home. Never. We will be foreigners for ever. . . .'

Mummy looks at me as if she sees me for the first time. She picks up the sheet of paper and lets it slide through the narrow slit of the slightly open table drawer. 'Let's have some potato soup.'

She rises to her feet and puts the pot on the stove. I place a few sticks of kindling wood in the stove and light a crumpled piece of newspaper under the wood. The crackling sound of fire mingles with the scraping of the spoon as Mummy stirs the soup. Silently she ladles the steaming liquid into two white enamel bowls.

The warm soup stills my anguish. Neither of us speaks but we know a truce has been reached. We also know that the terms are open to negotiation. Except one, a basic, non-negotiable principle: the three of us shall never be separated again. And so we would wait for Bubi's return at the weekend and the three of us decide together. It is one future for the three of us.

When Bubi comes home for the weekend, the three of us talk. And talk. I present my case with renewed passion. Sober voices prevail. Practical voices prevail. The majority wins. And by the end of the weekend the decision to go to America is final.

America, will you be my home?

The Statue of Liberty

At dawn on 7 April 1951, Mother and I stand on the deck of the *General Stewart* as it approaches New York harbour. On the horizon the hazy outline of a statue precipitates out of the fog.

'Look, Mummy, it's the Statue of Liberty!'

I grip her arm and point, wild with excitement. 'There. There! Can you see it, Mummy?'

'I can. Very well,' Mummy says, and her voice falters. She points in the direction of the statue as it continues to emerge from the morning mist. 'There it is . . .'

I swallow hard. A cheer rings out from the other refugees along the rails.

'Can someone sing the American anthem?' I cry out. 'Who knows the American anthem?'

No one seems to know the anthem of our new homeland. The words of the Israeli anthem reverberate in my mind, and I begin to sing, in Hebrew: '*Od lo avda tikvatenu* . . . Our hope is not lost, To be a free nation in our land, The land of Zion and Jerusalem.'

Several men whip off their caps and begin to sing. Women and children join in. Different anthems. In different languages. A cacophony of voices ripple the foggy dawn.

My heart is brimming. I look around. The deck of the refugee boat is full now. A mass of faces, full of awe and anticipation, focused on the Statue of Liberty as the boat chugs past it. The *grande dame* of our dreams now rises resplendent against the first rays of the sun.

Mummy turns to me and says, 'Let's go, Elli, and gather our things. We shouldn't be among the last ones to step ashore.'

I nod. 'Let's be among the first.'

APPENDIX A

Our Family During the Holocaust: Chronicle of Events

SEPTEMBER 1938   Hungarian troops occupy Šamorin, my hometown in Czechoslovakia, and rename it Somorja

NOVEMBER 1938   Hungarian authorities order our business closed

MAY 1940   Hungarian authorities confiscate the merchandise from our business

AUGUST 1943   My brother leaves home to attend the Jewish Teachers' Seminary in Budapest

OCTOBER 1943–MAY 1944   The Hungarian military police stage 'raids' on our home. My father is arrested and subjected to torture called 'interrogation'

19 MARCH 1944   German troops invade Budapest, the capital of Hungary. The rest of the country is unaware of this development. My brother comes home but my parents advise him to return to Budapest

21 MARCH 1944   The country is stunned by the news of the German invasion. Jews are arrested on the streets of Budapest and put on trains to concentration camps in Germany. My brother reaches home for the second time

25 MARCH 1944   All schools are closed. Our teacher dismisses us without explanation

27 MARCH 1944   The Jewish residents are ordered to deliver all jewellery, radios, and vehicles to the Hungarian authorities. I have to part with my brand new bike. My father takes me down to the cellar and points out the spot where he has buried our jewellery

28 MARCH 1944   The Jewish residents are ordered to wear a yellow star and paint a yellow star on their homes

3 APRIL 1944   Report cards are distributed in the schools. I receive the class honour scroll

5 APRIL 1944   Jews are forbidden to communicate with their Gentile neighbours

18 APRIL 1944   The Jews of Somorja are deported to a ghetto in Nagymagyar

14 MAY 1944   My father is taken away to a Hungarian forced-labour camp

17 MAY 1944   All books, documents, holy scrolls are burned. I save the notebook with my poems

18 MAY 1944   Beards are shaved off

21 MAY 1944   Ghetto Nagymagyar is liquidated. We are taken to Ghetto Dunaszerdahely. I give the notebook with my poems to a young Hungarian soldier for safekeeping

27 MAY 1944   Ghetto Dunaszerdahely is liquidated. We are put into cattle trucks

31 MAY 1944   We arrive in Auschwitz. I am separated from my

brother and my aunt Serena. Aunt Serena is killed in the gas chamber

10 JUNE 1944   We are taken to Camp Plaszow

5 AUGUST 1944   Camp Plaszow is evacuated. We are put on trains to Auschwitz

8 AUGUST 1944   We arrive in Auschwitz. A number is tattooed on our left arms. My mother is injured, and becomes an invalid

9 AUGUST 1944   My mother is taken to the infirmary

30 AUGUST 1944   With the help of friends I smuggle my mother out of the infirmary

1 SEPTEMBER 1944   We stand for selection. I am put in the transport for the gas chamber. I escape and join my mother on the transport for Augsburg

3 SEPTEMBER 1944   Mother and I arrive in Augsburg in a transport of five hundred women

3–4 APRIL 1945   We are taken to Mühldorf, then Mother and I are transferred to Waldlager. In Waldlager we meet my brother across the barbed wire fence

24 APRIL 1945   Mühldorf/Waldlager is evacuated. We are put on to a train

27 APRIL 1945   We are mistakenly released from the train, then recaptured. Mother and I meet my brother along the train tracks. We are driven back into the train. The three of us remain together

28 APRIL 1945   The train of prisoners is attacked by the US Air Force near Poking

30 APRIL 1945   We are liberated from the trains by the US Army at the Seeshaupt train station in Bavaria

7 MAY 1945   Germany surrenders. Church bells ring

MID-MAY 1945   We are taken to Flack Kaserne, a transit camp near Munich

MID-JUNE 1945   We arrive back in Somorja, now called Šamorin, my hometown in Czechoslovakia

JULY 1945   We receive news of my father's death

SEPTEMBER 1945   I am back at school. My mother, brother and I make preparations to emigrate to the USA.

APPENDIX B

Significant Historical Chronology

30 JANUARY 1933   Adolf Hitler is appointed Chancellor of Germany

15 SEPTEMBER 1935   Citizenship and racial laws are announced at Nazi party rally in Nüremberg

13 MARCH 1938   Austria is annexed by Germany

9–10 NOVEMBER 1938   *Kristallnacht*: Nazis burn synagogues and loot Jewish homes and businesses in nationwide pogroms called

'Kristallnacht' ('Night of Broken Glass'). Nearly 30,000 German and Austrian Jewish men are deported to concentration camps. Many Jewish women are jailed

15 MARCH 1939   German troops invade Czechoslovakia

1 SEPTEMBER 1939   Germany invades Poland. Second World War begins

3 SEPTEMBER 1939   Britain enters the War against Germany

22 JUNE 1941   German army invades the Soviet Union. The *Einsatzgruppen*, mobile killing squads, begin mass murder of Jews, Gypsies, and Communist leaders

7 DECEMBER 1941   Japan attacks Pearl Harbor

11 DECEMBER 1941   Germany declares war on the United States

20 JANUARY 1942   Wannsee Conference: Nazi government leaders meet at Wannsee near Berlin to discuss the plan for the mass murder of Jews, called 'the final solution to the Jewish Question'

1942   Nazi 'extermination' camps located in occupied Poland at Auschwitz-Birkenau, Treblinka, Belzec and Majdanek-Lublin begin mass murder of Jews in gas chambers

19 APRIL–16 MAY 1943   Jews in the Warsaw ghetto stage an uprising

19 MARCH 1944   German troops occupy Hungary

15 MAY–9 JULY 1944   Over 430,000 Hungarian Jews are deported to Auschwitz-Birkenau where most are killed in gas chambers

6 JUNE 1944   D-Day: Allied powers invade western Europe

20 JULY 1944   German officers fail in their attempt to assassinate Hitler

17 JANUARY 1945   Death march: Nazis evacuate Auschwitz and drive prisoners on foot towards Germany. Large numbers die *en route*

27 JANUARY 1945   Soviet troops enter Auschwitz

15 APRIL 1945   British troops liberate Bergen-Belsen, and US troops liberate Dachau, Buchenwald, Mauthausen and other concentration camps

30 APRIL 1945   Hitler commits suicide

7 MAY 1945   Germany surrenders. The war ends in Europe

NOVEMBER 1945–OCTOBER 1946   War crime trials are held at Nüremberg, Germany

GLOSSARY OF TERMS

Appellplatz – ah-PELL-plahtz – central square of camp (literally, place of roll call) – GERMAN

Auschwitz – OWSH-vits – concentration camp located in what is now Os'wieçim, Poland

Blockälteste – BLOCK-ell-tess-teh – head of barracks (literally, block elder) – GERMAN

Dunajska Streda – DU-nice-kah STREH-dah – town in Slovakia

Dunaszerdahely – DU-nah-SER-day-hay – Hungarian name for Dunajska Streda

Ellike – ELL-I-keh – diminutive, affectionate form of name Elli; Ellikém, my little Elli – HUNGARIAN

Hasid – hah-SID – member of a pious Jewish sect – HEBREW

Heil Hitler! – hile HIT-ler – Hail, Hitler! – GERMAN

Herr Offizier – hair aw-fee-Tseer – Sir Officer (proper usage in addressing German military staff) – GERMAN

Kapo – KAH-poh – head of work detail – GERMAN, from Italian *capo*, head

Kommando – koh-MAHN-doh – work detail – GERMAN

Lagerälteste – LAH-ger-ELL-tess-teh – head of camp (literally, camp elder) – GERMAN

Liebling – LEEP-ling – sweetheart – GERMAN

Liquidation – LIK-vee-dah-TSIOHN – dissolution, slang for extermination, killing – GERMAN

Lódz – loodg or lahts – city in central Poland

Los! – lohss – Get going! – GERMAN

marschieren – mar-Shee-ren – to march – GERMAN

Oberscharführer – OH-ber-shahr-FEE-rer – senior platoon leader (military rank) – GERMAN

Planierung – plah-NEER-oong – levelling of ground – GERMAN

Plaszow – PLAH-shov – concentration camp near Krakow, Poland

Raus! – rowss – Get out! – GERMAN

razzia – police raid – HUNGARIAN, originally from Arabic

Revier – reh-VEER – infirmary – GERMAN

Ruhe! – ROO-eh – Quiet! – GERMAN

Šamorin – Shaw-mawrin – town in northeastern Hungary

Schutzstaffel – SHUTZ-shtah-fell – élite military and police unit of the Nazi party (literally, protective squadron) – GERMAN

Shaharit – shah-khah-REET – morning prayer – HEBREW

shiva – SHIH-vuh – seven-day period of mourning in Jewish religious practice – HEBREW

Somorja – Shaw-mawr-yaw – Hungarian name for Šamorin

SS – Ess-ESS – *see* Schutzstaffel

Tattersall – TAT-ter-sawl – London horse market founded by horseman Richard Tattersall

Weltschmerz – VELT-shmairts – sadness about the world's evils (literally, world pain) – GERMAN

Zählappell – TSAIL-ah-PELL – roll call – GERMAN